# THERE IS LIFE AFTER TRAGEDY

GOD'S PATHWAY TO HEALING FOR
DEEPLY WOUNDED SOULS

Sarah Jane Kellogg

*Sarah Jane Kellogg*

WESTBOW
PRESS®
A DIVISION OF THOMAS NELSON
& ZONDERVAN

WestBow Press books may be ordered through booksellers or by contacting:

WestBow Press
A Division of Thomas Nelson & Zondervan
1663 Liberty Drive
Bloomington, IN 47403
www.westbowpress.com
844-714-3454

ISBN: 978-1-6642-6809-8 (sc)
ISBN: 978-1-6642-6810-4 (hc)
ISBN: 978-1-6642-6811-1 (e)

Library of Congress Control Number: 2022910358

Print information available on the last page.

WestBow Press rev. date: 08/17/2022

*This book is dedicated to Zane Deiter, George "Buzzy" Parker, and Carolyn Ellebracht for opening their hearts and sharing their memories.*

# CONTENTS

Acknowledgments . . . . . . . . . . . . . . . . . . . . . . . . ix
Foreword . . . . . . . . . . . . . . . . . . . . . . . . . . . . xi
Introduction . . . . . . . . . . . . . . . . . . . . . . . . . . xv

Chapter 1    The Tragedy . . . . . . . . . . . . . . . . . . . 1
Chapter 2    The Gathering . . . . . . . . . . . . . . . . . . 12
Chapter 3    The History . . . . . . . . . . . . . . . . . . . 19
Chapter 4    The Family I Knew . . . . . . . . . . . . . . . . 25
Chapter 5    The Grandparents I Never Knew . . . . . . . . . . 37
Chapter 6    The Aftermath . . . . . . . . . . . . . . . . . . 46
Chapter 7    The Survivors . . . . . . . . . . . . . . . . . . 55
Chapter 8    The Purpose . . . . . . . . . . . . . . . . . . . 64
Chapter 9    The Wounds . . . . . . . . . . . . . . . . . . . 74
Chapter 10   The Triumph . . . . . . . . . . . . . . . . . . . 84
Chapter 11   The Exchange . . . . . . . . . . . . . . . . . . 93
Chapter 12   The Legacy . . . . . . . . . . . . . . . . . . . 105
Chapter 13   The End . . . . . . . . . . . . . . . . . . . . . 114
Chapter 14   The Conclusion . . . . . . . . . . . . . . . . . 125

Appendix A: The History: The Long Version . . . . . . . . . . 129
Endnotes . . . . . . . . . . . . . . . . . . . . . . . . . . . 137

# ACKNOWLEDGMENTS

———

I want to thank the many individuals who helped make this book possible. To my first cousins—Zane Deiter, Buzzy Parker, and Carolyn Ellebracht—who shared both happy and painful memories with me, I am eternally grateful. Without their accounts of the tragedy from so many years ago, there would not have been enough information to piece this story together. In a real sense, they gave me *grandparents*. I am also grateful to other family members for their continued support during this project, especially Elaine Notario. She was my mainstay always checking on me and encouraging me to press forward.

I'm grateful to my first cousin Gene Bode for the amazing book he self-published that covered much of my family's history—*If the Bench Could Talk: Fifty Years at Bode's.* There were also the unpublished manuscripts of my greater family history compiled by Sadie Olene (Walker) Barrett and her daughter, Karen Eileen (Barrett) Craig Lerma, which were beyond helpful. Their work was nothing short of finding a gold mine.

I would also like to thank my editor, Karen Davis Hill, for her great insights into my writing style and the enormous help she was in shaping my book to be the best that it could be. And my heartfelt thanks also go to my publishing team at WestBow Press who gave me courage and confidence from the very beginning of the publishing process.

———

# FOREWORD

---

In 2002, I became the pastor of the First Baptist Church in Claremore, Oklahoma. Very soon after getting settled into our ministry, I met a couple who was going through a difficult time. Ed and Janie Kellogg were fighting the battle for Ed's life. Cancer had invaded their very existence, and unless the Lord had another plan, Ed would soon see the face of our sweet Savior.

As their pastor, it was my honor to walk through Ed's homegoing and Janie's beginning of a new life as a widow. I soon became aware that Janie Kellogg was no nominal believer. She was a true follower of Jesus Christ.

I hope you as a reader will allow me to refer to Sarah Jane Kellogg, the author of *There Is Life after Tragedy*, as Janie. As her pastor, I knew her as Janie. She was loved at the First Baptist Church as Janie. She is, at this very moment, my longtime friend Janie. When you read her book, you are going to become her friend. You are going to see her deep walk with the Lord. And she will become more than an author of a wonderful book; she will become Janie.

Let me make an understatement: Life is filled with tragedies! Some of these experiences are quiet and unknown. Some of them are open for the world to see. Tragedy takes the breath out of us. Tragedy dominates our lives and many times prevents us from taking a step forward. With every tragedy, the people walking through the situation always ask, "Will we ever get through this? Is there ever going to be a day, or even a moment, when I smile again? Is God there? Is there really a purpose to what I am experiencing?"

The answer to these questions and a thousand more can be found in *There Is Life after Tragedy*. Sarah Jane Kellogg has let the reader into the

---

depths of her life. You will read about a family tragedy suppressed for many years. It will be your delight to see how that experience changed the lives of many people for their good and for the glory of God.

*There Is Life after Tragedy* is a book of hope. The tragedies of your life do not have to strangle you every day. The difficult experiences you are walking through today do not have to be the end of joy. The hard days on your calendar can be turned to days of praise by the strength of the Lord.

Sarah Jane Kellogg's book will cause you to reevaluate your tragedies in life. You will find yourself looking for the blessings of the Lord rather than the defeats of the experience. Read every word. Read every page. The Lord is getting ready to show you *there is life after tragedy.*

Dr. Ted Kersh
Ted Kersh Ministries
Edmond, Oklahoma

*All the hard places in our past are but rungs on the ladder*
*that got us to where we are today.*
*Without them, we can never rise*
*to a higher place in God.*

# INTRODUCTION

———

"Why wouldn't you just leave it buried?" asked my doctor friend when I told him I was writing a book about my family's tragedy—a story that had gone silent for more than seven decades. His response unnerved me.

I knew I would have to deal with that question sooner or later, and sooner came quickly. As I left his office and walked to my car, thoughts of uncertainty filled my mind. Why wouldn't I leave it buried? Why was I unearthing something my father and his siblings had chosen to leave hidden—at least for their lifetimes? Had their choice been intentional, or was it simply a natural result of cautious training of their minds not to go there?

In my book, *There Is Life after Tragedy,* I explain why I chose to uncover my family's tragedy even though it came with challenges. It is a heartbreaking story—the kind that wounds the soul. There are several viewpoints of this event, including the story as seen through the young eyes of my first cousins—those personally involved—and the story as seen through the eyes of those who watched from the sidelines—neighbors, townspeople, and extended family members. But there is yet another story that has compelled me to write this book, and that is God's story.

We need look no farther than the greatest book ever written—the Bible—to recognize that many ordinary men and women were used to tell God's story of the lost and found, of bondage and freedom, of defeat and victory, and yes, of death and life. Through all of history, we see God Himself reaching out to everyday people so that He might include us in His all-loving plan for humanity. Only as my family's story can be God's story, am I willing to put into print what others chose to leave unpublished. That is the very crux of my intent to unearth the story that God wrote through my family's lives, be it joyful or immensely painful.

———

You will read about Bible characters who faced tragedy as well as people who are alive today. These stories confirm that you aren't alone in dealing with tragedy's staggering effects on your life. My greatest hope for you is that you will be able to find God's story in your own tragedy and begin to see your experience through a new perspective—God's perspective.

I have included my family's history that dates back as far as the 1300s. The short version is located in chapter 3, and the longer version is found in appendix A. Unfortunately, we are living in a time when character and courage are being defamed, monuments of heroes are being defaced, and medals of honor are being disallowed. Yet unless we remember them and spare the history of the brave souls who lived it, we are in danger of losing sight of who we are. Their ancient stories will remind us why history matters to us and our posterity.

I have expanded my family's tragedy beyond what had been known for more than seven decades to include the inner turmoil of those most impacted. The survivors' lives were rearranged, and nothing would ever be the same for any of them. Or would it? We hear news coverage of tragedies about people we don't know and give little thought to how they actually put their lives back together—or better yet, how they managed to get out of bed the next morning.

I have also included personal encounters with the painful losses in my own life. Oh, not nearly as tragic as those of my relatives, but painful just the same. I journaled throughout the years of dealing with my husband's fierce battle with cancer and eventual death, my lost identity, and aloneness. I have sprinkled my own insights on coping with loss throughout the book simply because they fit.

The psalms speak deeply to our hearts as we read about those who put into writing the agony of their own ravaged hearts. King David is one of my heroes because he was brave, vulnerable, and transparent as he shared his innermost feelings of pain and fear. We hear him crying out to God to come to his rescue. I have also cried out to God to rescue me, and I suspect that you have as well.

It is the gut-wrenching experiences we live through that shape us into the people we are today, transforming us into pliable instruments in the hands of the Heavenly Potter. Through my own hard trials, I came to believe that out of the anguish of the soul—my mind, will, and emotions— revelation is birthed (comes to life). It is those very experiences that become the spiritual fibers of our Christian faith on which we hang our hope.

The hymn writer William T. Sleeper, in his song "Out of My Bondage, Sorrow, and Night,"[1] points us to the discovery of God's great story. The lyrics tell of coming out of hard things, like bondage, sorrow, and dark nights, and coming into the victorious things, such as freedom, gladness, and the light that Jesus offers to us. At the end of the verse, the hymnist makes this firm declaration: "Jesus! I come to Thee!"

There it is. *There is God's story!*

Coming out—coming in!

Coming *out* of hardship, sorrow, and night and coming *in* to a glorious life!

We must come out *before* we can come in!

And if we never come in, we will never grasp God's story!

God is always leading His children to a better place. There is a clear directive in the pathway God has for each of us—out of hard things and into better things. Even the deeply wounded among us can find His plan for healing and recovery woven into our stories of tragedy and loss. The prophet Jeremiah wrote, "'For I know the plans I have for you,' says the LORD. 'They are plans for good and not for disaster, to give you a future and a hope'" (Jeremiah 29:11 NLT).

It benefits us to remember that the trajectory in God's stories always points in the same direction. Even though that road bends and twists through difficult circumstances, over high and seemingly impassable mountains, and down through deep and dark valleys of despair, it will eventually lead us all to the same grand place. *It leads us home.*

My paraphrased version of 2 Corinthians 3:18 written by the apostle Paul goes like this:

> God's children are all being changed to look and act like our Savior—we are all moving in that same direction—one change in us after another, from one glorious image to yet another increasingly glorious image—always moving us in the direction of Christlikeness. Until slowly but surely, we will at last find ourselves home with God.

And that, my friend, is God's story in all of our lives, including my grandparents, Oscar and Ethel Bode, and all five of their children.

# CHAPTER ONE

# THE TRAGEDY

Some people spend a lifetime sorting through the *whys* in life. For Leo Bode, that lifetime seemed like an eternity, a forever of finding no answers—only more questions. Darkness met him around every corner and under every stone upturned. The myriad of strange voices in his head grew louder with each passing day. Try as he may, he found no relief.

As a young man in his late teens, my uncle Leo went to a dance in a nearby town on a Saturday night. Dances were one of the few forms of entertainment for young people in the 1930s. As he got out of his pickup truck, he found himself in the middle of a fight already in progress. When the police arrived, Leo was mistaken as being a part of the fight. A full account was never officially recorded, but the sketchy pieces of the puzzle included a law officer acting in haste, a blackjack wielded in error, and a damaging blow to Leo's head that altered his life forever.

When he began having seizures, his parents, Oscar and Ethel Bode, told family members, friends, and neighbors that the seizures were genetic. The truth about what happened to Leo at the dance that night was part of the family secrets kept hidden away. Leo never dated and married but continued to live at home with his parents. Any efforts to find solutions through medical help were unsuccessful. One doctor's report described him as "having frontal headaches, vertigo, and a loss of memory … The attacks varied in severity and duration, and produce a great deal of nervousness at times. He had frequent pains deep behind the bridge of his nose." The problem was that the doctor attributed these symptoms to an attack of influenza and treated him accordingly.

Leo was later diagnosed with mental issues, even though little was known about mental health issues in the 1930s and 1940s. Limited, if any, scientific research had been completed at the time. Modern medications that are successful today in curtailing excitable and volatile behavior were still undiscovered. The most common solution was to place an individual suffering from such a disorder in a mental institution. Leo was taken to a state mental facility in Abilene, Texas.

Regardless of the conditions where Leo was placed, he did not like being in an institution. He would call his mother and beg her to let him come home. Her mother's heart would break, and finally, she would succumb to his pleas. Leo would live at home for a time, but only until his parents could no longer handle him. Then he would be returned to the facility. Eventually, Leo ran away from the facility and hitchhiked home. No efforts were made to return him again.

It is little wonder that Ethel struggled with sending Leo back to an institution that didn't offer any solutions for her son. Basically, there was no help, no medication, and no treatment for Leo. For the last seventeen years of Leo's life, his parents lived with this son who was normal 95 percent of the time and who suffered with uncontrollable seizures 5 percent of the time. It would be that 5 percent that would eventually cause them great alarm.

Leo occupied his time with a fascination of guns. He was somewhat of a gun expert and repaired them for other people. He was also talented with his hands and made jewelry out of silver dollars. Leo was a big man, and his strength was a blessing to the family on several occasions—one being when his sister's home caught fire. A fire from the fireplace had broken out in the attic. Leo climbed up into the attic and his brother-in-law carried buckets of water and handled them up to him. Bucket after bucket, they were able to keep the fire under control until the fire department arrived.

Leo enjoyed life with his two brothers, hunting with them and helping them when he was needed. He often helped with projects around their farms and ranches, things like fence building, shearing sheep, and working cattle.

Leo was a part of a big, happy family of sisters, brothers, in-laws, and nieces and nephews. His niece said that when she was a little girl, he kept a supply of chewing gum on the frame above the door in her grandmother's home. Leo would hike her up onto his shoulders and hold her up to the doorway so she could get a piece of gum.

However, the nieces and nephews were afraid of their uncle when he would have a seizure. Being at their grandparents' home often, they witnessed his seizures many times. They wouldn't know what was happening to him, so they ran away to hide in the first place they could find—usually the large garden close to the house. Peeking through the tall stalks of corn, they watched and waited. The one thing they knew for certain was that Uncle Leo's behavior was very different from the rest of the family.

His increasingly bizarre behavior became daunting to all family members. The doctors had failed; the mental institution had failed. His parents' only hope for their son to be normal again was a divine healing from God. He had been prayed for many times, but the miracle they needed didn't come. One Sunday night at church, Leo walked to the front and asked for prayer for himself. Several church members and family members gathered around and prayed with him.

"No one knows what is going on inside my head," Leo told those who prayed for him.

The struggle was unimaginable, the stress snowballing with each day that passed. Oscar and Ethel finally admitted to their adult children that they were afraid of him and were locking their bedroom door at night. Ethel made a shocking statement to her daughter. "I'd rather be dead than lock him away somewhere." It was profound to say the least, if not prophetic.

She could not have possibly known the full impact of her weighty words, spoken only days before the unthinkable happened. The signs were there in plain sight—an injury to the head, inaccurate diagnosis, the wrong medical treatment, and missed opportunities to help someone who tried desperately to find a way to remedy the struggle going on inside his mind.

## A Dark Day—June 25, 1946

Ethel enjoyed the cool, southerly breeze blowing in her face as she hung a load of laundry outside on the clothesline. Oscar's bib overalls, Leo's jeans, and some work shirts were soon flapping in the wind. This day was no different from any other day on a quiet ranch in the Texas Hill Country, where folks worked hard to make a living and minded their own business.

The morning hours were filled with her usual housekeeping chores, washing, and putting away the fresh vegetables Oscar had brought in from the garden. She anticipated what to make for dinner. In 1946 in rural Texas, the noon meal was called "dinner" and was the main meal of the day. The evening meal would be referred to as "supper" to these country folks, and it mostly consisted of leftovers from dinner. Ethel decided on making a large pot of Southern gumbo full of freshly dug potatoes and green onions, to which she would add just-picked tomatoes and whole okra pods. There would be more than enough for the two of them and Leo, who was working on guns in his shed out back.

Ethel was well-known for making large pots of food, as she often cooked for her grown children and grandchildren. The Bode family had made many fond memories around their large, round, oak table. Their dining room had become a place of lively conversation sprinkled with much joy and laughter. It was a long-standing family tradition, after the meal was over and the dishes cleared from the table, that the adults would push back their chairs, relax, and discuss the events in the church, the community, the nation, and the world.

When the family had finished the noonday meal, Oscar moved into the living room for a short rest. Just as he did every day, Oscar pulled off his shoes, reclined on the sofa, and soon fell asleep.

After washing, drying, and putting away the dishes, Ethel decided to wash her hair in the kitchen sink. She removed the clip holding up her long, dark hair and repeatedly brushed through it. She was too preoccupied to notice when Leo entered the kitchen carrying a gun. With sheer determination as if carrying out an order, Leo shot his mother several times before she fell to the floor. If Ethel had been given a chance to plea for her life, it was to no avail. The scene indicated some sort of struggle took place, but the facts would never be known. Her dead body fell between the living room and dining room of the small house. Ethel died right there—in the same kitchen and dining room where she had spent a lifetime cooking and serving those she loved, including this beloved son.

Oscar was awakened by the shots in the kitchen. As quickly as his fifty-six-year-old body could move, he ran barefoot for his life. Out the front door and through the yard gate, he headed for his Willis pickup truck in the detached garage. Being an expert rifleman, Leo shot and killed his father before he could reach the garage. Bullet casings were found on the sidewalk outside the front door of the house. Oscar's body was facedown a few feet beyond the yard fence.

In only a matter of minutes, Leo had carried out the heinous actions that had plagued him for hours, for weeks, and perhaps for years. It had happened methodically, just as he had imagined it in his befuddled mind. Those dreadful, tormenting thoughts, which had kept him awake night after night, had won the struggle within. It was done. Perhaps the demons would now leave him alone.

On this day, Leo did what he had always done after having a seizure. He went to bed to sleep it off. He slept for several hours before waking to find the devastation from his actions earlier in the afternoon. Once he realized the carnage he had done, he determined to take his own life. The sheer agony of living with his actions—these actions—wasn't an option for him at this juncture. Leo ran down the road less than a mile, and there he cut his own throat and shot himself in the head. His body was found approximately four hundred yards from the house with his .25–.35 caliber rifle nearby. He had taken double measures to ensure that he would not live—not after this.

The dead bodies of Oscar, Ethel, and Leo would not be discovered for three days in the blistering Texas sun that was typical in late June. On Wednesday night, their daughter Hallis told her husband that she was missing her parents as she had not seen them since Sunday. Carlos suggested that she and the children drive over to visit them and perhaps spend the night. But because it was already late in the evening, Hallis decided to wait until the next day, which would have been Thursday.

At 8:30 the next morning, before Hallis and her two children had left for their visit to the grandparents' home, the discovery at the Bode residence had already been made. Was this happenstance or the hand of God that kept this daughter and two grandchildren from being the first to arrive at the horrific scene? No one knew for sure, but they were grateful nonetheless.

Neighbor Ray Bierschwale and daughter, Pauline, were driving past the Bode home, using a well-traveled shortcut through the Bodes' property. They were on their way to Harper, the small town where folks in this community bought groceries, gasoline, and other necessities. Ray first noticed Oscar's body on the ground and instantly knew that some sort of disaster had taken place. He sent his daughter on down the road to a neighbor's house, where she could call for help. As she made her way in the direction of the neighbor's house, she came upon the dead body of Leo. Pauline reached the neighbor's house and called officials, informing them that something was very wrong at the Bodes' home.

The local newspaper reported that "the Bodes had last been seen in Harper on Monday, and it is believed that the tragedy occurred early the next morning."[1] However, one neighbor told investigators about hearing several shots around 4:30 p.m. that same day. He thought nothing of it since farm folks shooting guns for whatever reason was a common occurrence. He had no reason whatsoever to go and check it out.

As best they could, family members along with Kerr County officials attempted to put together the puzzle pieces of what might have happened to this normally quiet and peaceful family. Their final conclusion was that thirty-five-year-old Leo was repairing a gun when he suffered a seizure—much like the seizures he had experienced many times in the past. Apparently, this time he was unable to control himself and had succumbed to the horrendous thoughts that plagued him for years. The only difference in this day and other days is that today he carried them out.

## Discovering the Carnage

Floy Bode, the oldest son in the Bode family, was the first family member to receive the terrifying call. He got in his pickup truck and quickly drove the seven-mile trip to his parents' home, having little concept of the horror that awaited him. Shortly before Floy died of cancer in 1990, some forty-five years later, he shared brief details of that dreadful day with his daughter Elaine. His words came forth slowly as he struggled to form the sounds. Drawing deep breaths between his short, uneven phrases, Floy described finding three-day-old dead bodies that were hardly recognizable. Not only had the one-hundred-degree days taken their toll, but the small, wild animals had ravaged their bodies. He saw detestable vultures—filling their role in the ecosystem of all living things—waiting in the background. Except for the location where the bodies were found and the familiar clothing, they looked nothing like those of the three family members Floy knew and loved.

First he came upon the mutilated body of his brother. Next he would find the body of his highly respected father—now dark brown and swollen—a sight never to be forgotten. Lastly, he entered the ranch house where he saw the bullet-ridden body of his mother on the floor of the kitchen. As his voice broke with emotion, Floy muttered words to Elaine, describing the sights that no son or brother should ever have to face.

It was some time before officials arrived at the scene. When they did, they found Floy walking in circles—his arms wrapped around his chest—and groaning. Words were not heard, nor were they needed. Pain to this extreme could not be verbalized, not spoken, not muttered—just groaned from the depths of one's soul.

All roads leading to the property were barricaded, allowing no one to enter. Even family members were refused entry. For those charged with working this crime scene, it would be months and years before the images would not haunt them—if ever.

The coroner's verdict was that Oscar and Ethel Bode died at the hands of their son and that their son then committed suicide. The headlines in many local papers spread across south Texas described the tragedy and shock over the course of the next few days. But newspaper headlines are merely an attempt to reduce an unthinkable tragedy into as few of words as possible, for the sake of printing space. They can never tell all—accurately describe injured souls in printed form. They are simply facts or details that are intended to shock and gain readers' attention. They certainly felt heartless, cold, and indifferent. Little, if any, thought is given to the wounded—the survivors, as they call them. What a strange word for deeply wounded people. Who knew if any of them would actually *survive?*

"Harper Family of 3 Discovered Dead on Ranch"[2]
"Officers Seek Clue to Triple Tragedy"[3]
"Farm Family Is Shot to Death"[4]
"Harper Mourns Tragic Death of Bodes in Triple Slaying"[5]
"Three Members of Family Found Shot"[6]
"Triple Funeral Services Were Held Here Saturday"[7]
"Funeral Services Held for Bode Family Saturday"[8]

Shock and grief have their own way of defying reality. This is one of those things that happens somewhere else—not in a small, safe, quiet community like Harper, Texas. It happens to people you *don't* know—not to people you grew up with, loved and respected. It happens anywhere but *here* in your world. Yet it did happen here. It was up close and personal— reality in its truest form. An elderly father and mother, four adult children and their spouses, six grandchildren, aunts, uncles, brothers, sisters, nieces, nephews, and cousins, along with hundreds of friends and church family, would have to find a way to cope with this tragic loss of life and love. It would be some time before anyone recovered, and perhaps some would not recover at all.

## Saying Goodbye

Triple funerals—all together on the same day. Triple caskets—could a family bear more than that? Can life lost be reduced to a four-foot by six-foot box or three four-foot by six-foot boxes? Exponentially—rapidly becoming greater in size—clearly defines the scene. Grief multiplied somehow seems harder. Does anyone remotely know where to start to bury the grief, the shock, the pain, the past? Sure, others have been there; it's just different when the loss is yours.

One thing was certain; there had been no time to prearrange any of it. It now had to be done off the cuff, spare of the moment, with no time for do-overs. And who among the hurting could even think straight? Could any of this be the unseen hand of the Heavenly One this family served? Would God—their parents' God—help these shell-shocked adult children now? Was He even here in this strange, new place they now found themselves—gut-wrenching pain they had never before thought about much less experienced? Or had they even thought about pain before today? Would they be paralyzed by a pain they didn't know existed? Their family history tells stories of challenges, hardships, loss of life, and yes, pain. Yet making sense of it all would have to wait. There were more pressing issues—and a triple funeral to plan and attend. After all, we all leave here the same way. Well, mostly.

Walking through days of grief in a state of shock is much like sleepwalking: you're not in control and you don't know where you're going. You just walk. You walk because you have to and because others expect you to. Things have to be done—decisions, arrangements, purchases, and details, details, details. Yet how do you condense three lives into one memorial service? Can you cover fifty-six years, fifty-five years, and thirty-five years of living in only a few hours? That is a total of 146 years of down-to-earth living, 53,290 working days and sleeping nights, meals around a family table, hugs, hopes, and holidays. Who will ensure that you do it right—accomplishments, honor, respect, admiration—all deserved? Lives well-lived can't be diminished into too little space. There must be room to tell all that is important, show all, and acknowledge all.

Two thousand people, reported one newspaper, filed into the small Texas town with hardly room to park a few hundred cars. Yet a sea of cars squeezed their way into yards, into driveways, between buildings, and on sidewalks. People were standing everywhere, since one small-town Methodist church could barely hold a good-sized grieving family.

In her book *The Way of Abundance*, author Ann Voskamp reminds us of a familiar Bible story in the book of John where Jesus encountered a man who was born blind. The disciples wanted to know who had sinned: the man or his parents. Jesus answered them, "You're asking the wrong question. You're looking for someone to blame. There is no such cause-effect here."[9] "This happened so the power of God could be seen in him."[10]

Jesus's disciples were looking for answers. Isn't that what we all want? We need to blame someone thinking that perhaps it will relieve our pain. A cause-and-effect response could seriously help us cope. At least we think so. But we don't hear any sort of reasonableness embedded in Jesus's answer. No, none whatsoever. What we do hear is a rather shocking statement that

God had a higher plan than we expected: a plan that would turn the focus on Him and His power. That's all. You mean that is it? It doesn't make sense to our small earthly thinking, but even beyond that, we still cannot see anything positive in such brokenness. God would have to show them, and like everything God does, He isn't in a hurry.

The road ahead would be crooked, veering around steep and narrow places, attempting to avoid gigantic rocks clearly in the pathway to healing—healing of a pain that refuses to go away. So painful that no one would talk about it even decades later—not until every member of the immediate family had departed this life. And that was their choice—a choice that had been respected.

Ann Voskamp's words cause me to think beyond what I have ever imagined about pain or brokenness. Is it because we all focus so much on getting over the pain that we fail to see the intent of God that was right there all along? In her amazing poetic style, she continues.

> There's brokenness that's not about blame. There's brokenness that makes a canvas for God's light to be lavishly splashed across the darkness. There's brokenness that carves windows straight into our souls. Brokenness cracks open a soul so the power of God can crack the darkness of the world.[11]

Light versus darkness—isn't that what God's plan has always been about? We were flung into darkness the day our earliest ancestors ate the forbidden fruit in the Garden of Eden, and ever since, God has looked for ways to get light into our dark world. We need light to survive. We need light to find our way. What we need more than anything is the Light of the World. If we can accept it, God's bigger and higher plan is always greater than our immediate need.

*The dark clouds overhead do not diminish the presence of God. They just keep us from seeing Him for a while.*

One thing was certain for this family: light was needed simply to take another step. And for now, none of them knew what that next step would be. Yet as with any hard trial, the dark clouds overhead do not diminish the presence of God. They just keep us from seeing Him for a while.

His glory will yet appear to us again.

> We have been in many trials, but we have never yet been where we could not find all we needed in our God.[12] — Charles Spurgeon

# CHAPTER TWO

# THE GATHERING

The cattle-guard entrance to my cousin's ranch home rattled both my car and my nerves. For the hundredth time, I questioned if I knew what I was doing. I was no stranger to anxiety, and feeling my heart throbbing inside reminded me how awkward this whole thing could be. I was certain that my blood pressure was on the rise. Realizing it was too late to back out now, I breathed a prayer that I was right where I was supposed to be.

My cousin Elaine and I had arranged this meeting of the first cousins in our family to discuss the grandparents we had never known. Both Elaine and my older brother were too young to remember them, and their untimely death occurred before my sister and I were born. While our oldest cousins had agreed to attend the meeting, I had little confidence that anyone actually wanted to open this can of worms.

My grandparents' deaths were a subject that had been taboo, at least until today. As a child, I believed a made up story about them being killed in an automobile accident. When I learned the truth later in life, I knew by instinct that asking questions was not an option. What little information I had gained in my entire life came from Elaine's mother, who being a daughter-in-law to my grandparents was perhaps the only immediate family member able to discuss it at all.

Deep inside I was afraid we were crossing a line—asking to discuss something no one wanted to revisit. Yet I had prayerfully done my homework, calling each cousin who had recollection of our grandparents and asking if they would approve of such a gathering. Two cousins told me it was all right to have the meeting, but they wouldn't be there. Their hesitancy melted over time, but not without some refreshed pain. I never intended for the decades-old event to once again cause pain. Hadn't it already caused a lifetime of pain? To think I was responsible for its reoccurrence was more than I could bear.

In the weeks prior to today, I continually reminded myself of how I got here in the first place—planning an unwanted meeting. But why had I taken the risk? The idea had emerged on the day of my aunt's funeral—the last remaining child of my grandparents. Elaine and I discussed how our parents, aunts, and uncles had been such strong people down through the years and protected us from the effects of the tragedy. We wished for a way to honor them—for their courage, resilience, and ability to persevere through such sorrow.

In that same discussion, we discovered that neither of us knew much about the tragedy itself, although Elaine knew more than I did. Before her father passed away, he had told her just enough about his parents' demise to increase her longing for more. Yet her chances for gaining information from her immediate family were now gone. Two years earlier, her only sibling had passed away, and her mother had recently been diagnosed with dementia.

Hearing the pain in her voice, I asked what I could do to help.

"You can write our family's story," she responded without hesitation.

I reluctantly agreed, knowing full well the difficulty of what she had asked of me. Together, we had approached this idea of meeting with our older cousins to discuss the issue. In time, they had all agreed to attend. And today was the day.

My husband, Owen, and I had made the eight-hour trip to my family's hometown just a few days before. Coming to the Texas Hill Country had always been a highlight in my life. My aunts and uncles had served as grandparents for me and my siblings, and my older cousins each held some sort of hero/heroine status in my life. To visit here was almost magical, something I had looked forward to from my earliest recollection.

But today—well, maybe not so much. I had done my best to prepare for this gathering—my opening comments about why we were here, my questions, and most of all, my heart. My laptop, printer-scanner-copier, and notepads were carefully tucked away in the back of my car in the event I needed them. Taking a deep breath, I slowly got out of the car, took my husband by the hand, and walked to the door.

When the door opened, we were engulfed in hugs and handshakes. Why had I doubted that we would be met with anything less than their usual south Texas-style hospitality? Everyone arrived over the next thirty minutes, and more hugs were exchanged. It had been a few years since I had seen them, and the delight I felt inside was sweet and calming. I gladly welcomed the lightheartedness as we caught up on each other's families, health issues, and of course, grandkids. It seemed like any ordinary family gathering and my uneasiness of what was to come subsided, at least for the moment.

My cousin Carolyn had opened her charming home on the outskirts of Fredericksburg for our meeting. Not having seen it before, I was given the grand tour. It was a sight to behold—a fully refurbished German-style home built in 1880 and made of twelve-inch-thick stone walls inside and out. I marveled at its history as she escorted me from room to room, sharing the details as we went. The twelve-foot-high ceilings gave it a look and feel of true elegance. The large porch wrapped around three sides of the home, inviting visitors to stop and rest in one of the welcoming wicker chairs. Thriving potted plants adorned the porch with Southern beauty— gorgeous blue and lavender hydrangeas that reminded me of the cover on the latest issue of *Better Homes and Gardens* magazine. They also reminded me that I can't grow those beauties in Oklahoma. I had tried.

No important gathering in Texas can happen without barbecue, potato salad, and all the fixings. Today was no exception. We piled our plates high and enjoyed lively conversation around the oversized table in the family dining room. There was room to spare for the ten of us who had come for this unusual gathering. When it was time for dessert, we were served a banana cake made from our grandmother's recipe book. Those of us who had never had the chance to taste our grandmother's cooking would do so today. With each bite I savored, I longed for more—more recipes, more stories, more memories—that would tell me about my grandmother.

Did she love music as much as I do? Did she sing? Did she like to cook? Was she like one of my two aunts, one of my cousins, my sister, or me? And my grandfather—was he like my dad, my uncle, or maybe my brother? Did he love children? Did he play with the grandkids? Do any of us look like either of them?

There was this enormous *need* to know churning inside me—maybe not as much a need as a want. I truly longed to know. Those untold secrets of many years ago had remained secret far too long. What might I learn from these three cousins who had been between eight and eleven years old at the time of the tragedy? Would I be glad to know what they were about to say? Or would I be disappointed and regret that I had asked? Only time would tell.

## Information Download

As the dishes were cleared from the table, the time had arrived for the very purpose of this gathering: to discuss our grandparents and the terrible fate that befell them. One by one, our spouses slipped away to another room, leaving the blood kin cousins to talk. Sitting around that big dining table, right there in open daylight, three brave souls set out to discuss a dark day back in 1946.

Zane, the oldest of the first cousins, sat across the table from me. She had been eleven years old at the time of the tragedy. She was born in our grandparents' home and lived with them for a period of time. To my right, on one end of the table, sat her brother, George—better known as Buzzy—who was ten years old back in 1946. He had a memory as sharp as if it all happened yesterday. At the other end of the table sat Carolyn, our hostess for the day and the one who had baked the cake from our grandmother's recipe book. Carolyn had been only eight years old at the time of the tragedy. What these cousins knew was precisely what we had come here to find. Could their hearts bear up under the strain of their memories? If so, would our hearts be able hold it all?

I forgot all about my prepared notes—my preface to start the meeting. After stumbling through a few botched sentences, I put caution aside and opened my heart and mind to receive. I breathed a quick prayer that my brain would engage and retain what was about to be downloaded on me.

During the next few hours, the secrets I had longed to hear began to unfold. I tried taking notes, but it soon became an overwhelming task. It seemed as though a dam had broken and pent-up water gushed forth across a newly opened pathway. Each cousin patiently waited for his or her turn to talk, but one story led to another as an avalanche of information spilled out, story after story. Sweet memories, mingled with tears and laughter, flowed freely as they recalled all the good things about our shared grandparents. Memories once buried deep found life again.

My cousins had also come prepared. They brought pictures in weathered frames, some with curled edges and others tarnished by a century of wear and tear. They were soon spread across that big dining room table along with yellowed newspaper articles, family Bibles, and wedding certificates. Carolyn retrieved a large, oval-framed picture of my grandmother as a young girl. It hung on the wall of the lovely entryway of her home. So many photographs and trinkets—things we didn't know existed—were brought out one by one. There was even an invoice from the local funeral home for multiple caskets. All of these things provided real evidence that my grandparents had indeed lived, loved, and yes, tragically died.

As the youngest granddaughter, who had long believed a lie about their deaths, I had barely seen a group photograph of these strangers. My soul swelled with emotion as I remembered feeling betrayed by the made-up story. Still, I knew in my heart it was some measure to protect me from the darkness my parents had endured. I suppose some hard things are better left unsaid lest they shatter a child's trust in the goodness of God or man.

But on this day, I felt great gratitude to God for bringing me here and to my cousins for their selflessness in imparting to us what they knew. It had taken great courage on their part, as it had not been easy for them to get here.

It was a new space for all of us. Months later, I realized we had made an extraordinary exchange on that day, though the benefits to each of us wouldn't be known for some time. Yet it happened. One summer afternoon in June, my cousins—now in their 80s—opened up their hearts at the risk of opening their wounds. They shared freely as God's ointment of grace poured forth covering us all.

## Back Home in Oklahoma

In the days following my arrival back home in Oklahoma, I began sorting through all I had seen and heard during our meeting. The undertaking ahead of me seemed nearly impossible. There was too much information to gather in one, two, three, or perhaps more meetings—*too little* family history to trace without massive research. And many family members had already passed away.

Too much, too little, and was I up to the task? Was I the right person to write this story—their story? I had little experience: no books published and a few published articles, though none noteworthy. There is my eight-year-old internet blog—180 posts of raw and unchallenged thoughts. At the very bottom of my unimpressive resume rest my annual Christmas letters that I've written for over twenty years. I am pretty sure they don't count, although one business professional told me he had a collection of them that he kept in his sock drawer. *Seriously,* there is no significant writing to my credit.

My confidence waned. Could I do justice to my cousins' pain—the pain of tragedy that I had not known? Yet having buried a mother, a father, and a husband, I did know something about the unanswerable questions that scream for answers, the reoccurring dreams that won't stop coming, and the tormenting *whys* that linger until one pleads for numbness. I had heard the voices seeking to comfort say, "Time heals everything," knowing full well that it's a lie. And the comments intended to uplift. "You'll come through this stronger." "You'll come through this with more faith." The best one hopes and prays for is that you'll come through it at all.

Still, I had not faced tragedy. I had not walked the paths engulfed in thick darkness that tragedy carries with it. I clearly had not held jagged-edged pieces of broken life in my hands and attempted to put them back together again—some that will never fit—*ever*. The landscape of my three cousins' young lives had been changed, and my ability to capture their story was questionable. Feeling the weight of the project before me, I penned this prayer in my journal.

> You are God on the good days, and You are God on the bad days.
> You are God when Your children live long, fruitful lives, and You are God when tragedy cuts life short.
> You are God when we have plenty, and You are God when we lack enough.

You are God when we have good health, and You are God in our sicknesses.
You are God when we are happy, and You are God in our sorrows.
You are God when we understand, and You are God when we don't.
You are God.
Period.

In the days, weeks, and months that followed, my confidence in myself continued to waver. There was a distance to go before I could feel like I had feet under me. Almost a full year passed before I sat down to the task—a year of doubting myself to write the story and my willingness to tread unchartered waters. If the written story was ever to become a reality, it would have to happen by the will and grace of God.

It would also have to happen because these three first cousins were willing to open their hearts and tell me what they knew. I fully respected

*Sometimes God holds our hurts and pains captive until they yield their treasures to our lives.*

the fact that this astronomical task of unwrapping the past would not be easy for them. Yet it had to be this way since I had no knowledge of my grandparents whatsoever. It would literally be a look back for them into the good times and the bad times and to be forthcoming with what they knew. The only way I could write this story would be through their eyes.

Sometimes God holds our hurts and pains captive until they yield their treasures to our lives. Only time would tell if we could, in fact, uncover those treasures.

Dear God, Your will, nothing more, nothing less, nothing else. Amen.[1] —Bobby Richardson

CHAPTER THREE

—

# THE HISTORY

I returned home from the gathering with my first cousins with mixed emotions—a lot of gratefulness for their generosity in sharing but also a bit of anxiety over the stash of documents, affidavits, articles, and pictures I had brought home with me. All the names and places ran together in my mind.

My ancestry was somewhat documented, and I certainly had dozens of leads to research, but it would take many hours to piece it all together. My son, Brent, was intrigued by the thought of having *nobility* in his background, so he began to do research as well. He helped me discover some of the treasures.

My intent in this chapter is to give only a short overview of my family's history. A more complete and detailed account is documented in the longer version in appendix A of this book. If you like history, you will enjoy reading it.

## History Matters

Some families have roots that run deep. Mine is one of those. While readers often view it as boring, I like to think of history as looking in a rearview mirror. You're not going that way, but it does give you a small glimpse of where you've been. History tells us much about how we got to here, and it will likely give us clues about where we'll be in the future. With the availability of ancestry web sites today, people can easily research where they came from. However, for some it can be encouraging, while others wish they had left that stone unturned.

It is our family story that most clearly defines who we are as a people—rich or poor, strong or weak, proud or humble, good or not-so-good, religious or nonreligious—all characteristics that describe our group, those people called by our last name. My dad's family surname is *Bode*, a German name for which we have known roots in Germany as far back as the mid-1800s.

A larger number of Germans came to America during the early colonial years for various reasons—one being the advantage of free land

*I like to think of history as looking in a rearview mirror. You're not going that way, but it does give you a small glimpse of where you've been.*

as German religious groups were being suppressed by their government just as those in England. The ones who came thought relocation to a new land was the only solution. By the time of the American Revolution, nearly 200,000 Germans had settled in New England states—mainly Pennsylvania. These were called the "Pennsylvania Dutch." Later, in the middle of the 1800s, another group of immigrants from Germany made their way to the shores of America, settling in the Midwest. They had left Germany because of political turmoil and agricultural failures. It is believed there were as many as 1.5 million Germans who came during that era, of which my ancestors were a part.[1]

## The Bode Family Roots

Many families who migrated from Germany settled in what is known today as the Texas Hill Country, making up a large part of the pioneer population of the area. This is where my ancestors eventually settled.

For six long weeks this group was on the water looking anxiously for the new land of which they had heard. On July 26, 1855, they landed at Indianola, a small harbor about thirty miles due south of Victoria, Texas. Among the possessions that they brought with them were two iron wheel wagons. At Indianola they bought a yoke of oxen and started out in search for their new home in the adopted land.[2]

The growing family moved several times settling north of Castell in Mason County near the mountains later known as Bode Peaks. After a short period, they moved to Cold Creek in Llano County. In 1872, the family returned to Mason County, about eight miles northwest of Castell, and established their final home. Their children married and began families of their own, developing a settlement that was called Bodeville. Few, if any, family members currently live there.[3]

For many generations, the Bode family made their living by farming and ranching. Like most folks in those days, they had strong work ethics coupled with strong faith in God. It took both to survive the hardships of life in unchartered territory. The Bodes were Methodist, being converts of the Martin Luther Reformation era.

In 1889, Paul Otto Bode married my great-grandmother, Anna Radetzky. The Radetzky family dates back as far as the eleventh century and has a colorful history.

## The Radetzky Family Roots

The Radetzky family descended from an ancient Czech (Bohemian) family of nobility. An account of their history is more fully documented in appendix A, including the story of the famous Joseph Wenzel Anton Radetzky, who was a Bohemian nobleman and Austrian field marshal. He was greatly recognized and honored for his valiant and loyal service. He retired at age ninety and was immortalized by Johann Strauss I's "Radetzky March." The march became an unofficial Austrian national anthem.[4]

My great-grandmother, Anna, was born in Germany to William and Susanna Radetzky. The couple had six children, three of which died in infancy. With their three remaining children—daughters Marie and Anna and son, Frederick William, they migrated from Prussia and settled in Bodeville, Texas, in May 1884. Anna was eleven years old.

Bodeville is where my great-grandparents, Paul Otto Bode and Anna Radetzky, met and married. Paul and Anna Bode had a total of twelve children, three of whom died in infancy. Their oldest son was my grandfather, Oscar Robert Bode, who was born in October 1889. He was followed by eight siblings: Selma (Bode) McDonald, Aurora (Bode) Barker,

Reseda (Bode) Walker, Reuben Bode, Elgin Bode, Milton "Bill" Bode, Forrest Bode, and Clifford Bode.[5]

Throughout my childhood years, I knew and loved many of these relatives and played with their children and grandchildren. The annual Paul and Anna Bode reunion made that possible. I also remember going to the home of my dad's uncle Clifford Bode to visit my elderly great-grandmother, Anna, in the 1960s. At that young age, I was clueless about her rich history spanning two continents. I can only hope that someone captured her story before she left this earth in 1966, but if they did, I do not know about it.

These great-grandparents moved to Harper, Texas, a small town in Gillespie County, in 1901. There my grandfather, Oscar Robert Bode, met my grandmother, Ethel Iva McDonald. Ethel was the daughter of William Augustus McDonald and Louanna Elizabeth (Lacy) McDonald, who are my maternal great-grandparents and have interesting family histories.

## The McDonald Family Roots

The McDonalds migrated to Texas from Illinois and were among the earliest pioneers who came to the Hill Country. As early as the 1850s, the McDonald frontiersmen helped establish various settlements, including Harper as well as an area west of Fredericksburg, a well-known and visited German-style town and tourist attraction today. One of the most popular tourist sites located in Fredericksburg's backyard is called the Willow City Loop, and it has spectacular fields of bluebonnets—the state flower of Texas.

Pioneers Eli and Caroline McDonald and their children were part of the tragedy that occurred in August 1864, in which Eli lost his life. His wife and five children were taken captive and held for many months. Their story is one of hardship and suffering.

Today, the sight known as the McDonald Massacre is officially marked by a Texas Historical Marker on the east side of Harper. These early settlers lived in constant fear, and several lost their lives protecting their families, homes, and livestock.

Another story of tragedy that occurred in the McDonald family was that of Lafe McDonald's wife, Alwilda, and her mother, Mrs. Wiley Joy, who lost their lives at Banta Branch. No doubt, life on the Texas frontier was filled with adversity, fears, and yes, tragedy.[6]

## The Lacy (Lacey) Family Roots

My maternal great-grandmother's family was named Lacy. Her family history traces back to that of William Lacy and Elliott Lacy. A more detailed description of the Lacy family is included in appendix A.

The descendants of William Lacy stretch from Georgia to Texas and include a Miss America, Mary Ann Mobley, from Mississippi in 1958. Drury Lacy, son of William, founded a dynasty and was vice president of Hampden-Sydney College, where many of his offspring received their education. They became doctors, ministers, missionaries, soldiers, and politicians.

There were law men and outlaws, con men and cons, Texas Rangers and enemy fighters. Lacys have served their country in every major war from the Revolutionary War to Vietnam, some making the supreme sacrifice. They were officers and enlisted men, army, navy, air force and marines. The Lacy women were missionaries, doctors, teachers, and homemakers. Pioneer women worked beside their husbands, and in some cases raised large families, too.[7]

## Faithful and Brave

My family history is indeed noted by admirable deeds and grand titles such as nobility, coat of arms, knights, barons and baroness, count and countess, church founders, royal chamberlain, empress, nobleman, field marshal, viceroy, statues, memorials, marches, pioneers, dynasty, college founders, well-known ministers, sweet singers of Israel, and high-ranking officers and military men.

My first thought is *Oh my, such a high bar has been raised for those of us who follow them!* And I suspect that they had footsteps laid before them just as we do, even if we don't have records of their names, who they married, or the dates when they lived. Nonetheless, they were there—living, loving, giving, and dying faithfully and bravely. I am inspired by the words of the song recorded by Steve Green titled "Find Us Faithful."[8] The writer, Jon

Mohr, says the footprints that we leave on earth will indeed impact the lives of those who follow us. The hope is that we will be faithful to leave them a clear pathway that leads to God.

As I have sifted through the books, documents, records, newspaper articles, and numerous personal testimonies, I found that their footprints did, in fact, lead me to God. What I have discovered has unlocked some of the secrets of my past and has been worth every minute of research. While the grand titles of nobility were exciting to read about, there were other things of lesser significance that spoke more deeply to why I am *me*.

My heart has genuinely been stirred to strive harder to leave more than material things to my children and grandchildren. There are the riches of faith and faithfulness that I desire for them to embrace. There is great wealth found in nobility of character and strength and a good name to uphold. There is such value in honesty, kindness, goodness, and compassion that reflect the heart of the God my family has served for centuries.

It is the desire of my heart that all who come behind *me* will have found *me* faithful as well. We must never forget that history matters.

> The patterns you set will form a pathway that others will walk.[9] —Priscilla Shirer

# CHAPTER FOUR

# THE FAMILY I KNEW

My hometown, Harper, is located in the very center of Texas. The rugged hills of granite and limestone are sparsely covered in yucca and cactus plants that intermingle with beautiful live oak trees. From my earliest childhood days, I remember the hundreds, or perhaps thousands, of windmills and concrete water tanks strewn across the endless acres of farm and ranch country. Traveling over the hilly, winding, farm-to-market highways marked by low-water crossing, one could spot sheep and goats grazing alongside the longhorns and other robust cattle breeds. While the area is widely known for its extremely hot afternoons, the fortunate residents wake each morning to a cool breeze that has made its way from the Gulf of Mexico.

When I was a small child, my parents left Texas and relocated in southeastern Oklahoma. To return to my hometown for family visits or holidays was like a trip to heaven since we had three sets of aunts and uncles who filled the role of grandparents for my brother, my sister, and me. They made our visits there somewhat magical for the three of us, yet after I grew up, I realized it wasn't magic at all. It was simply their way of life.

Each set of aunts and uncles was unique. One couple lived in town and owned a business—a totally new experience for a little country girl. Frequent trips to my uncle's gasoline station for free candy and an orange crush soda pop were addictive. Another couple lived on a ranch where we had to cross the Little Devil's River, overlooked by a tall rock ravine. Driving through the low-water crossing of crystal-clear water was a thrill. Their house had an upstairs floor—the dream of every little girl. Last but not least, the final couple's house had a bathroom shower (totally unheard of in those days) and a swinging door between the kitchen and dining room. So much about their homes was unique compared to anything I had ever seen before.

Two of my relatives' houses had upright pianos that kept me entertained for hours. Nothing in the world could have made me happier. Most Texas ranches had concrete water storage tanks, something equal to an above ground swimming pool in your backyard. Each of their houses had one or more wood fireplaces, and we were carefully tutored on how a real live Santa would come down the chimney on Christmas Eve. In the Hill Country— well noted as a hunting paradise—most houses were adorned with mounted deer heads that had been killed on their ranches. So it was with my family— big mounts, little mounts, and unusual mounts everywhere! That was just how they did things in Texas. Everything Texans do is *big*. So magical was the only way this little girl saw any of their way of life.

If there had ever been anything strange or unusual that happened in the lives of my Texas family, I didn't know about it. They were all loving, kind, and generous. My religious roots sprouted in my uncle Carlos Parker's Pentecostal church, which delighted me just to visit there on occasion. The way I saw it—and them—was they were some of the happiest people on earth. After all, they had more than the necessities of life, like concrete water tanks and bathroom showers. Through my childhood eyes, these people were nothing less than perfect and had always been perfect.

Their existence was a direct result of the grandparents I never knew: Oscar and Ethel Bode, who brought a total of five children—three boys and two girls—into the world: Floy Bode, Leo Bode, Hallis (Bode) Parker, Cecil Bode (my dad), and LaVerne (Bode) Parker. Except for Leo Bode, who had died before I was born, these people were my immediate family and those who made my life meaningful. They bridged the gap left by my grandparents' tragic end. These loveable relatives filled our holidays, birthdays, summer vacations, reunions, and everything in between with love, laughter, and good memories. In short, they were my life—the Bode family I knew from my earliest recollection.

## Floy and Virginia Bode

Oscar and Ethel's oldest son, Floy, attended business college right out of high school. Afterward, he worked as a rancher in various locations and in time leased the Vallier Ranch, where he met his future wife, Virginia Vallier. They had one son, Gene Bode, and one daughter, Elaine Notario. Floy eventually went into business for himself in Harper. He owned and operated Bode Feed and Seed Store on Main Street, which included a gasoline filling station and a TV repair service for many years. He had handled much livestock and studied how to doctor most any ailment they might have, so he also became the local veterinarian for the community. He was a successful businessman for over fifty years.

Virginia was the hardest working woman I ever met. Perhaps hard work was all she knew since her father had left her mother with two young children and pregnant with a third child to raise by herself. Money was hard to come by in those days, so they scraped by anyway they could, such as raising chickens and selling eggs. Virginia told stories of being able to see light through the cracks in their dilapidated home. Life required hard work from every member of the family.

After marrying Floy, Virginia cared for her family, grew a garden, tended to all that needed doing around the house, and still found time to cook in the school lunchroom. I remember so many wonderful dinners served around the big, round table in their dining room. I later learned that big, round table had once belonged to my grandparents. Virginia was the only person in the family who ever told me anything about those grandparents. I was in my midforties when she and my uncle came to visit us in Oklahoma. She opened up and talked about my grandparents, yet the tragedy was never mentioned.

Floy was a trusted and respected person by the entire town. People in that era were not yet trusting of bankers, so my uncle was asked by many folks to keep their money for them. He set up a record for each, and when they came to town, they would go by his place of business to get some of their money to buy groceries and other supplies. Before they returned home, they took what was left back to him to keep until their next trip to town.

In his book *If the Bench Could Talk: Fifty Years at Bode's,* Gene described his father.

He was a very efficient, self-made person, capable of doing most anything from shoeing and breaking horses to setting up his own and the Harper School's record books; from carpentering to mapping out the Community Cemetery; from doctoring an old cow to sitting on any board of community affairs. He grew up chopping and picking cotton and raising livestock which gave him the ability to think for himself and evaluate most situations; always honest, standing tall, and always willing to be of service to the public.[1]

Floy also belonged to the local fire department, and he often acted as a first responder when a call for help came. He was no stranger to injuries or to death, as pain and suffering are simply part of life in a small community.

Gene was unquestionably the businessman cousin. He took over his dad's business when Floy retired and took the business to the next level, expanding into the popular game feeding industry. He was as much a businessman as his dad. He married a girl from Missouri and twice each year they would travel to St. Louis to visit her parents and stop at our house in Oklahoma along the way. It was obvious that Gene adored my dad. He was a delightful and true big cousin.

Gene's sister Elaine was the smart cousin and the first cousin to graduate from college. She was closer in age to my sister and me than all of the other cousins, so we had more in common. Not that we saw each other that much, but it sure was fun when we did. She was a high school girl and then a college girl, and my sister and I were fascinated with her. I will always remember my first formal dress. I needed a dress for my eighth-grade graduation so Aunt Virginia mailed a dress to me that Elaine had worn to some fancy school affair. To me it was the most beautiful dress in the world. Whatever Elaine did or had was amazing to us; even her old 1957 Plymouth with big fins in the back seemed like a classy Mustang, Elaine's future dream car. When she graduated from college, she finally bought that gold Mustang with a black top that she had dreamed of owning someday.

Gene and Elaine also had an amazing maternal grandmother, Jessie Vallier. Because these grandchildren had lost their paternal grandparents,

Mrs. Vallier gave them two Christmas presents and two birthday presents each year—one from her and one from the grandmother they had lost.

## Hallis and Carlos Parker

Oscar and Ethel's oldest daughter, Hallis, married a rambunctious young man by the name of Carlos Parker. As a young boy, Carlos was referred to as a "terror on wheels." That same enthusiasm carried over into his Christian faith as Carlos was considered a fiery Pentecostal preacher. Carlos and Hallis had one daughter, Zane Deiter, and one son, George "Buzzy" Parker. Carlos was instrumental in establishing and building the First Pentecostal Church of Harper. The church was a pillar of the gospel in the community and still stands today.

Both Zane and Buzzy were grown and out of the house during my childhood, but my recollection was that whenever we went to Texas for a visit, they were always at their parents' home. As far as I knew, they could have lived with them. They were very close and a part of those big Texas memories that I have tucked deep within my heart.

Zane was the charming cousin. I have always been fascinated with her accent, of which I have no clue where it came from. Her delightful stories, intermingled with her soft, enchanting laughter, are charming indeed. For years, my grandmother's upright piano sat in Hallis' living room. During my visits to their house, Zane taught me all she knew about playing the piano in one short visit every year. It was from her that I learned to play chords with my left hand. I still cherish the old Pentecostal hymnal that she wrote the chord charts in so I could learn them.

Years later, when I was twenty-three years old, Zane passed my grandmother's old upright piano on to me. I had yearned for a piano since I was a little girl, even using a paper keyboard at one time to learn how to read notes. This old piano that had belonged to a grandmother I didn't know now meant the world to me, yet all I knew about its history was that it had once belonged to her.

Then there was my cousin Buzzy—unquestionably the fun cousin always making people laugh. I've never seen him fail to spread smiles and laughter at every gathering. It is usually subtle and one-on-one so as not to draw attention to himself. He had his own special way of telling stories about pranks he and my cousin Gene had played on the older German gentlemen who were regular visitors at the Bode Feed Store where they both worked. Buzzy was an avid arrowhead hunter and spent his free hours digging for arrowheads in a field next to the Little Devil's River. He had a massive collection of arrowheads as a young man and has even more today. He is also known as the Harper historian, knowing the townspeople that he grew up around and their children for generations. He is never without an amusing story to tell from yesteryear.

Hallis was perhaps the best cook in Texas—for real! She ran her two-story, five-bedroom home much like a bed-and-breakfast, except that it was free and also came with lunch and dinner. There was hardly a week that went by that this generous couple didn't have guests in their home. Her kitchen had a breakfast nook with a built-in booth and benches. This cozy corner had windows on two sides that overlooked a beautiful flower bed in the well-groomed yard. A booth meant that when someone needed to get up, everyone on that side of the table had to file out as well. There is no way to count the number of people who at one time or perhaps many times were served coffee and homemade cookies in the little nook attached to her kitchen.

Uncle Carlos never met a stranger. He liked to talk as much as he liked to preach, and he invited everyone he struck up a conversation with to come to their home. I can still hear him say, "Y'all might as well come to the house because Hallis will have some supper cooked anyway." And it was true—she could roll out a delicious meal on a minute's notice. They had freezers filled with homemade Texas sausage that they processed themselves—beef, deer, and goat meat all carefully dressed in their tank house. Now a tank house is a rock building underneath a large water tank that holds the water pumped from a well with a windmill. It would always be cool inside and a perfect place to process meat. After all, this was Texas and Texans have their own way of doing things.

Their backyard was equipped with a long, concrete picnic table that seated at least twenty people. It was overlaid with Mexico tiles on the top and had concrete benches on either side. It was frequently used over the years to serve hundreds of guests a south Texas barbecue. Hallis would make the food inside, except for the meat that would come off the huge outside BBQ pit, and carry all the dishes out to a serving table. Texas iced tea—strong and sweet—was always served in colorful tin cups because it tasted better that way. Family gatherings, reunions, and even Oklahoma visitors were reason enough to call the relatives together to celebrate in their welcoming backyard.

Hallis' home was the first house I had ever seen with an upstairs floor. What little girl doesn't like to climb stairs? Oh, but these were special stairs—at first, anyway. But one may not have known the upstairs existed since the steps going up to it were hidden in the ceiling and had to be pulled down. It was several years before a full staircase was built. Carlos was also a carpenter; therefore, their house was in constant state of being remodeled. In their later years, they added on a large den, complete with a gigantic limestone rock fireplace, Mexico tile floors, and huge deer and elk mounts on all the walls.

*They were servants of the Lord who lived what they preached.*

Many years after I was grown and had a family of my own, Carlos and Hallis came to visit my family in Oklahoma. They wanted to spend a few days vacationing in Branson, Missouri, but didn't want to drive in that crowded tourist town. We were delighted to be the ones to take them.

While in Branson, we attended *The Andy Williams Show* in the magnificent Andy Williams Theatre. We made our way to our seats in this 2054-seat auditorium, somewhere about two-thirds of the way back from the stage. After sitting there for a few minutes, my aunt took a long, gazing look across the sea of people sitting below us, hundreds no doubt, and remarked, "Look at all those old people." She was correct in that most all of them were gray headed or had no hair at all. I thought it amusing, considering the fact that both my aunt and uncle were in their late seventies and Carlos had been bald since his early twenties. They just never saw themselves as old, mostly because they were so active. But if the old saying is true, "You are as young as you feel," these two were still young indeed.

After they returned to their home in Texas, my husband and I agreed that we had not heard one word of criticism or negative talk about anybody from either of them for the entire week. They were servants of the Lord who lived what they preached.

## Cecil and Della Bode

The youngest son of Oscar and Ethel was Cecil, who was my father and married to my mom, Della Mae Lang. They brought three children into the world: a son, Ronald Bode, and two daughters, Pamela Medcalf and me. My parents were living in California at the time my dad was drafted into the army near the end of World War II. He was shipped overseas and landed on the shores of Italy, where he engaged in combat. My dad told his nephews some of his most painful experiences, yet these were things he had never shared with his children. Unquestionably, those horrific scenes had left their mark on his life.

Upon returning from the war, my dad made his living as a cattle rancher. He spent his life in southeast Oklahoma, New Mexico, and south Texas, operating large ranches. At the peak of his career, he and my brother were featured in *The Cattleman Magazine* in September 1980, in an article titled "A Delicate Balance." The writer stated, "Cedar Springs Ranch [which my dad managed at the time], 12,500 acres of Kimble and Mason County land, supports not only what may be the largest commercial Angus operation in the Hill Country, it does it in harmony with its wildlife."[2]

In his book, Gene described my dad like this:

> "Uncle Ceese" took the place of my grandpaw. I learned from the man. I used to stay each summer with him. He would farm, ranch, carpenter, build fence and shear sheep. He would not half-do any job. If it wasn't done right, he would not do it at all. The man helped me every way he could. I can still see that neat smile and those shiny, bright eyes. He would always give that right hand a half-turn before it got to your hand for a handshake. I've been with him on lots of hound dog 'coon hunts. He liked the few people; quietness times. He loved good horses and good cattle, and knew how to handle both. I loved the man and he loved me. I miss him a lot.[3]

And speaking of good horses, my dad had a love affair with his horses. My grandfather, Oscar, and his father, Paul Bode, mail-ordered a mare from Germany. This mare, called Nellie, came across the Atlantic on a ship and provided our family with great offspring for many years. My dad's horses were all registered through the American Quarter Association, but he gradually began to breed his mares to Thoroughbreds. This meant they could run faster and for longer distances. Many Sunday afternoons were spent at horse racing tracks scattered around southeast Oklahoma. He never won a lot of money, but as a savvy businessman, he at least broke even. It did provide him with a sport that he enjoyed—that is, almost as much as running coon dogs.

One of the most valued gifts I was ever given was a two-year-old filly out of my dad's bloodline of horses. You would have thought Prissy was worth a million dollars because she certainly got the royal treatment. She was a pet and part of our family for sixteen years. During her entire lifetime, she was able to have only one colt, which died a week after birth. As if that wasn't enough of a loss, the next week, Prissy died from a twisted gut—a condition that the veterinarian could do nothing about. My loss was huge.

My mom, Della, was a full-blood German who learned to speak English when she started grade school. Since English wasn't her first language, she spoke slowly and methodically—and it was *always* kind. My mom was a full-time wife, mother, and homemaker. She grew the garden, canned the vegetables, made bread and clothes, washed clothes for her family on a wringer washer, and was an amazing cook. She was also a gracious hostess who fed her many guests like they were royals.

Because we lived so far away from my dad's siblings, they often traveled to Oklahoma to visit us. We never had a large house with extra bedrooms, but I remember my mom and dad rolling out the red carpet when family would come to visit. Sometimes it would be for a few days, and for others, it might be a week. My mom never complained but worked hard to see that they were comfortable and well fed.

"My dear Aunt Della … she was a very special person to me. She had a nice wit and super attitude. She was a loving and caring wife, mother, grandmother and friend, as well as an aunt to me. Left us way too early" was how my cousin Gene described her.[4]

My mom did leave us early—dying of cancer at age forty-eight. I was only twenty-one at the time, and as I look back over my life, I wonder how I managed to reach adulthood without her. Her graciousness is what I remember the most about my mom. There is an old adage that says, "You don't know what you have until it's gone." It is so true.

My brother, Ronald, was eighteen months old when our dad returned from the army. The story goes that my dad told my mom she had had her time with him, and now it was his turn. He promptly dressed him in Levi's jeans along with cowboy boots and a cowboy hat. They were inseparable from that day forward. Ronald was all the things a little sister could want—especially since I was a tomboy. He let me follow him around on the ranch, totally looking out for me. My brother is basically a younger version of my dad—you know, the perfectionist type. Ronnie, as most people call him, is well-loved for his mild mannerisms and his big smile. My love for him runs deep.

My sister, Pam, was the exact opposite of me, yet she was a perfect big sister in every way. She cooked and cleaned and made her momma proud. She was always smarter and prettier than me—having the perfect hair and the perfect skin—and was no bigger than a minute. Then there was me—her outgoing little sister who likely embarrassed her a thousand times. Even though she loved being indoors as much as I loved the outdoors, we still played together for hours on end. Pam and I both suffered a lot when our mom passed away so early in our lives. Somehow throughout the years, we found a way to be there for each other when our children were born, when Dad left us later on, and anytime life got difficult.

## LaVerne and J. H. "Son" Parker

The youngest daughter of Oscar and Ethel was LaVerne. She married J. H. Parker, better known as Son, and they had one daughter, Carolyn Ellebracht. They owned a large ranch in the Noxville Community north and west of Harper.

LaVerne was renamed Nonnie by her oldest niece. It seems that the family was calling LaVerne—Vernie for short. But two-year-old Zane couldn't quite manage the "V" and began pronouncing it "Nonnie. Whatever the reason, the name stuck and LaVerne was called Nonnie by family and friends alike. Aunt Nonnie had the sweetest voice I've ever heard—with no exceptions. I do not think it was possible for her to get loud. It just never happened. Her voice and her laughter were delightful. Just ask anyone who knew her.

A visit to Uncle Son and Aunt Nonnie's house was generally the last of the three stops that we made whenever we visited Harper. They had custom-built their home, and it was ahead of the times in home building. So many little things were built in, and much thought had been put into every detail. My sister and I could play in the front side of the house in the formal living room and dining room, and it was barely noticeable to those visiting in the back side of the house in the den, breakfast room, and kitchen. Fortunately for me, the piano was in the front part and I could play to my heart's content without bothering anyone else.

The fun at their house was offset by the teasing behavior of Uncle Son. He was a great big man when I was a really little girl. He would tell me that he liked "baby meat," as if he were a big, hungry bear, and then pretend to chase after me. Of course, I would scream and run away, generally to the car since it happened only as we were packed up and ready to leave. All the grown-ups were laughing, so I should have known that he was teasing. As we would drive away, I could hear him say something like "I'll get me some baby meat next time you come."

Their daughter, Carolyn, was my beautiful cousin. She added extra fun to our visits there by allowing us to sift through her old high school keepsakes that were stored in her former bedroom at her parents' home. She had been a twirler in high school, and her closet was full of memorabilia. My sister was much better at twirling the baton than me since I spent most of my time at the piano. To us, the school banners, pom-poms, and yearbooks were novelties because we had never seen anything like them.

Carolyn literally spent hours trying to teach me to swim in their concrete water tank. It never clicked for me, so I never got the hang of it. Actually, I might have if I could have practiced more than once a year. One summer she had a border collie puppy that stole my heart. She was looking for a good home for the pup and said I could have him. I could hardly believe my ears when my dad said I could take him back to Oklahoma. The dog rode between my legs in the floorboard of the back seat of the car. That may not sound strange today, but in those days, dogs didn't ride in the front of cars. They were supposed to ride in the back of pickup trucks.

Of course, my dad had an ulterior motive as he would train the dog to be a livestock dog. Our family loved and enjoyed him for many years.

Nonnie was perhaps the best cook in the world. I'm sure I said that very thing about Hallis, but then that it how it was—a toss-up between the two of them. Both were amazing cooks who had been taught to cook by their mother. She had also taught my dad to cook, and if he ever told me any tidbit about his mom, it was about being in the kitchen with her. My dad loved to cook and was good at it. I guess it just ran in the family.

That door between Nonnie's kitchen and huge dining room swung open many times as she put a lavish meal on the table. Leg of lamb—a rarity—was served with many fresh vegetables right from the garden she grew in her backyard. Who kept a garden clean enough to have it in your backyard? Aunt Nonnie. The vegetables were in the center, and the outside area was planted in beautiful flowers.

Because we saw these relatives so infrequently, many times when we would be at one of their homes for a meal they'd invite the other family members to come as well. It would end up being a big reunion with aunts, uncles, and cousins everywhere. They made my life feel whole, like I really hadn't missed anything by not having grandparents. After all, no one ever talked about my grandparents. It was as though they never existed. And if they had, I would have considered them my cousins' grandparents since I didn't have any.

> A life of faith is not a life of one glorious mountaintop experience after another, like soaring on eagles' wings, but is a life of day-in and day-out consistency; a life of walking without fainting.[5] —Oswald Chambers

# CHAPTER FIVE

# THE GRANDPARENTS
# I NEVER KNEW

In my early writing days, I had a wonderful mentor who was a teacher of English and creative writing at Rogers State University in Claremore, Oklahoma. She shared writing-skill books with me and reviewed some of my work. The thing I remember most was what she told me to do when writing about characters. "You have to make us love them enough to keep reading about them."

That is what I hope to do—make you love my relatives, the ones I knew and the ones I didn't. They were not famous or well-known, but they were immensely loveable people. It seems important to know who they were and what they were like in order to gain some understanding as to why their story was suppressed for many years—the story that broke so many hearts, threatened to shatter childhoods, and challenged everything any of them knew about God.

This account of my grandparents' lives was almost totally given to me by their three oldest grandchildren, with the exception of an amazing interview I did with Ruth Bode. Ruth was a sister-in-law to Oscar, having been married to his youngest brother, Clifford. At the time of my interview with her, she was the only living member of their generation. I had the honor of meeting with her two days before her one hundredth birthday in September 2019. As I talked with her and her son, Doug Bode, I found her mind to be clear and sharp as she told her story. My great-grandparents, Paul and Anna Bode, were at Ruth's home when the news of the tragedy came. Although it came as a devastating blow to the family, Ruth told me, "Leo lost his memory. It had been feared for some time that something like this could happen—considering Leo's seizures." When I asked her how the community reacted to the news, she commented, "Everyone expected something."

The process of my cousins imparting to me what they knew about our grandparents brought great joy to my life. I quickly learned to watch the expressions on their faces as they began to speak of their Bampa ("Băm-paw") and Nana ("Nă-naw"). Those expressions spoke louder than their words. Zane's and Carolyn's faces literally lit up as they brought forward those memories from so long ago. Their eyes sparkled as they spoke of little figurines, purses, and flowers. The tenderness of their grandparents' interactions with each of them was undeniable. Buzzy, who referred to himself as the ornery grandchild, fluctuated between tears and laughter as he shared from his heart. His moving stories were like treasures that had been lost for many years. As the stories were unpacked one by one, they unveiled for me these two loving and wonderful people we shared as grandparents.

One thing was certain as all three of them told their stories: each of them believed they were their grandparents' *favorite*. I have no doubt that they were. After all, who doesn't like to tell a grandparent story? And who doesn't like to hear a grandparent story? Each meeting, each phone call, and each story brought delight to me.

## Oscar and Ethel Bode

Oscar and Ethel started life together in 1908. Their first years of marriage were spent living in a tent beside the home of my maternal great-grandparents, the McDonalds. It has been said that "they had all the conveniences a tent home could afford."[1]

The couple's five children were born over the span of nine years. Like most Bodes, the family earned their living by raising livestock. They owned property west of Harper in the Reservation Community. To all who knew them, they were loved and respected and known for living a quiet and peaceful life.

Each person who described Oscar to me said he was a big, stout man—more than six feet tall with broad shoulders. My grandfather had big, blue eyes (like my dad), no hair, and wore a big hat. He mostly wore bib overalls, except when going to town, and then he dressed in khaki pants. Besides his livestock operation to earn the family living, Oscar spent many hours growing a large, beautiful garden. It was part of his daily routine to work in it every evening.

He was quite talkative and especially enjoyed listening to the radio while sitting in his big, wicker chair. He intently listened to news about the war while my dad was serving in the military overseas as well as radio preachers on Sundays. Oscar had a habit of pecking on the wooden arm of his chair with his favorite two-bladed, ranch-trapper pocketknife while listening to the radio. Today, that refinished chair sits in front of the fireplace in the living room at my aunt's home—with the dime-size circle of pecking marks well preserved.

The grandkids remember Bampa as being sweet and jolly, always loving and kind to the children. He both teased and spoiled them at the same time. Zane was the first grandchild, and her parents were living with her grandparents at the time she was born. She entered life six weeks early and weighed a mere three and a half pounds at birth, and she was a delight to their lives. Bampa was so tenderhearted that he cried the day she started to school. He was always a bit partial to the girls in the family, and it was no secret that he adored his youngest daughter, LaVerne.

When Bampa handed out money to the grandkids, he would give Zane a quarter, but to all the others, he would give a nickel. Since the others were younger, he thought they didn't know the difference. Buzzy said that he eventually figured it out when his sister could always buy more than he could.

The one and only story that I had heard about my grandfather was about the time when my dad was overseas during in World War II and my mom was living in an apartment in Harper. My brother was just a baby, and every time my grandparents came to town, they would stop by her apartment to see him. Oscar would head for the bedroom to get my brother, and my grandmother would tell him not to wake up the baby. But that didn't matter to Oscar. He would return from the bedroom each time carrying Ronnie in his arms.

My grandmother was described as "always loving and pleasing everyone." Like all women in those days, she wore nothing but dresses—to town, at home, and to work in the garden. She was an amazing cook making large pots of amazing food. She had big mixing bowls but also a set of bowls, saucers, and a blue pitcher that came free in oatmeal boxes. Carolyn watched her grandmother make "postem" (instead of coffee) and cereal for breakfast. Milk was kept in an ice cooler that required a block of ice once a week.

Zane especially remembers our grandmother making her gravy and cake icing. I'm sure they weren't eaten together, but those were her memories nonetheless. Buzzy, on the other hand, remembered the large cabbage casserole that she made and was often impatient waiting for the other family members to get to the table. Being the ornery child, he always wanted it *quick!*

Ethel loved her cats, and she loved them so much that she made gravy for them. She often watched through the kitchen window at the kittens playing outside. They made her laugh.

Another love of our grandmother's was flowers; she grew beautiful flowers. Every time Carolyn would leave Nana's house, Ethel would pick some flowers for her and wrap them in a wet rag to send them home with her. If Nana was coming to Carolyn's house for a visit, she would watch for wildflowers along the road and ask Oscar to stop and let her pick flowers to take to Carolyn. Today, Carolyn has a passionate love for flowers that she inherited it from her grandmother—as was obvious by those beautiful hydrangeas on her front porch.

Zane recalled an incident when she was four years old and Ethel was going out to feed the hunting dogs. Zane had wanted to go, but because it was so cold outside, Nana had said no. Zane went anyway. When Nana saw her, she gave Zane a little swat on the behind. Never having experienced such a dreadful thing in her entire life, she "almost died crying" as she described it. Her wailing over the swat was so loud that Bampa came outside to see what was happening, and of course, he came to her rescue.

The grandparents would regularly take the children to Fredericksburg shopping. They bought barbecue at Henke's, along with bread and pickles, and stopped somewhere under a tree to eat lunch. A trip to town always included a stop at Dooley's Five and Dime, where little toys and figurines were purchased. On rare occasions they would take the grandkids to Kerrville, a larger town in the area. That is where Bampa bought Zane a purse at Lehman's—a prized possession to a little girl in those days.

Zane loved telling a childhood story about her mother, Hallis. She didn't like washing dishes, but Ethel had her own special way of convincing her daughter to obey. When she refused, Ethel retrieved a sash from one of her dresses and tied Hallis to the bedpost. It wasn't long before Hallis had untied herself and hidden in her mother's clothes closet. To pay her mother back for the ill treatment, Hallis spit in all her mother's shoes. Who would have thought that she would grow up to be a pastor's wife?

One story about my dad when he was five years old describes my grandmother's wit, charm, and love for her children. My dad had two older brothers who made life miserable for him—just like most older brothers do. But one day when my dad was sick of it all, he decided to run away from home. He told his mom what he was thinking, and she helped him pack a small bag of things, made him a lunch, and helped him get on his horse. She waved and said goodbye as he rode away. She knew her son well, and just as she expected, he made a little trek down through their pasture, stopped to eat his lunch, and then rode his horse back to house. The whole ordeal was over in a couple of hours. My dad rarely spoke of his parents down through the years, except on occasion he would mention that he spent time with his mom in the kitchen where she taught him to cook. It was obvious to us that he loved her dearly.

## A Strong Faith in God

The Bodes were religious people and attended the Methodist church in Harper. Our great uncle, Willie Radetzky, was a circuit-riding Methodist preacher who rode on horseback from town to town preaching the Good News of the gospel of Jesus Christ. Buzzy remembered a sermon Willie preached at one of the Bode reunions. His text was Proverbs 22:1. "A good name is rather to be chosen than great riches." It was times like this one—spent with godly family members—that made such deep impressions on all of us. They were impressions that would shape our lives.

Somewhere along the way in the early 1930s, Oscar and Ethel were drawn to the Pentecostal Movement. My grandmother's sister, Carrie Calentine, along with three other women prayed for many years to have a Pentecostal church in Harper. As they were praying, God was listening, and He put into place an answer to their prayers.

The Lord moved on the heart of a preacher by the name of Hugh L. Watson to go to Harper and start a church. The first service was held in my great aunt's home. Although I didn't see it as a child, Aunt Carrie lived a hard and difficult life. Her husband left her with three kids to rear by herself. She did so by taking in washing and ironing for the public. Carrie's faith was strong and she never gave up on God. Her home became the hotel for all who came to minister at the church for years to come—and that was a lot of people.

The small group meeting for church in Carrie's home grew until a bigger place was needed. In 1931, a parcel of land was purchased from Charles Roberts on which to build a church. Charles was the grandfather of my uncle, Carlos Parker, who would become pastor of this church in future years. Many people, including Lemuel McDonald and his three sons, helped to put up the simple frame building with wood shaving scattered over a dirt floor. Instead of windows, openings were covered with solid wood shutters that could be propped open for light and ventilation. Pine pews were constructed, and the entire church was completed within less than a month. The building was dedicated by H. B. Taylor from San Antonio on March 23, 1931.[2]

The church experienced revival during the early years and members often prayed in the prayer room for two hours before services.

> There was a real demonstration of God's power in every service. This caused a great deal of curiosity in the whole community, and large crowds came to see what was happening. These were the days when no one minded staying until eleven or twelve o'clock every night praising and worshiping the Lord. As a result, there were people being added to the church daily. All the new converts were baptized in the Little Devil's River.[3]

The following chorus was written by Bill Guild for the early church in Harper:

Have you seen that place on Roberts Street called the tabernacle?
With the sawdust floors and soft-pine seats?
Down at the tabernacle.
O, precious is the place
Where I first saw His face.
No other place I know
Down at the tabernacle.[4]

Six pastors served the congregation during the next fifteen years. Many people were part of the growing church; however, in time, some moved away and the congregation dwindled to mostly women and children. When hard financial times fell on the church, Oscar and Ethel borrowed the money to pay off the church loan.

In 1931, Uncle Carlos was saved at that church. By his own testimony, he was deep in sin, had a drinking habit, and there was no one who could outcurse him. Carlos also heard the Lord's call to preach the gospel, and he began holding services in country schoolhouses and occasionally in neighboring towns. In 1948, Carlos became the full-time pastor at the First Pentecostal Church of Harper, and in 1949 he was instrumental in updating the small building. He bought the lumber and did the carpentry work to complete the interior. Although times were hard, their God always came through. He sent two couples from outside the church that covered the cost of the stone for the exterior of the building.

Later, an adjoining lot was acquired and the fellowship hall was constructed on it. Again in 1975, the church would undergo another complete overhaul with God giving Carlos the design for the refurbished building. The update included a cross, stained-glass windows, ceiling fans, etc. During the seventy-fifth anniversary celebration of the church in 2006, it was renamed the Lighthouse Fellowship Chapel. The church has continued to serve the community and share the gospel through the years.

My grandparents had been a major part in establishing this church. Of course, I knew none of this as a child. I had no idea of the history of the church, except that my family was there in a *big* way. Through the years, that church has been the place where my cousins got married and my aunts and uncles held fiftieth wedding anniversary celebrations, birthday celebrations, family Christmas gatherings, and family funerals. The funeral services for my parents were held there. Simply walking into the sanctuary brings back happy and sad memories all at the same time.

## A Love for Music

It was no secret that Oscar and Ethel's family loved music. It was part of who they were. It was known throughout the Reservation Community that if you heard a vehicle coming down the road with occupants singing at the top of their lungs, it was the Oscar Bode family going to town. All of the boys could play some kind of instrument. As a family, they would sit on the front porch and sing "Farther Along, When I Think of Jesus" and the grandkid's favorite, "The Birds upon the Treetop." Praising God in song is what they did. It was a lifestyle. They had songbooks dating back as far as 1894.

Hearing this story about my dad's family certainly rang true to my own upbringing. We also sat on the porch and sang at my home in Oklahoma. My dad could play the guitar and violin—better known to country folks as a fiddle. He taught my brother to play the guitar. My part was to sing lead, while my dad sang the harmony. It suited me just fine. There were many renditions of "You Are My Sunshine" and "Put Your Little Foot Right There." When I was old enough, my brother taught me to play the guitar. After he married, it was just my dad and me to carry on the family tradition of sitting on the porch late in the evening and singing every song we knew several times over.

*Praising God in song is what they did. It was a lifestyle.*

I suppose a love for music ran in the family. My grandmother's brother, Asiel Lafayette McDonald, spent much of his life teaching music. In the early 1900s, he created a music chart on oilcloth that measured five feet by seven feet with hand-painted musical notes. With his unique teaching tool, Lafayette taught both choirs and individuals how to read and follow notes.[5]

I will never forget Zane's words describing my grandparents. Her words reach deep into my inner being and encourage me to serve God the same way they did. Zane simply said, "The Lord was their life."

> Only as far as we can live Christ before the eyes of others can we help them to understand His message.[6]—Andrew Murray

CHAPTER SIX

---

# THE AFTERMATH

*A*ftermath sounds like an ugly word to me, yet I suppose it appropriately fits here in this story and in the lives of my family members after their tragedy. It may fit in your life as well. After all, don't we all have an after-*something* to deal with?

> After my husband's death—
> After the accident—
> After the surgery—
> After the breakup—
> After the divorce—
> After the kids left home—
> After the layoff—
> After the company folded—
> After the market crashed—
> After the friendship failed—
> After the hurricane, the flood, the tornado, the coronavirus—
> After the holidays—
> After, after, after—

I know you can relate—after that past, painful event that leaves one holding the bag, the empty nest, the empty bed, or the empty bank account. There's plenty of pain to go around in any one of those events that force us to face the "What's next for me?" question.

Stuff happens that is out of our control, and stuff happens to everyone. It isn't a matter of *if* but *when*. We are all a breath away from unexpected things happening to us.

Fortunately, not all unexpected things are as devastating as death. It is the finality of death that leaves us with no options. There is no patching things up, rebuilding the marriage or the house, or finding another job. Death is final, and there is no turning back, not even a detour. That is where tragedy places us—facing a future we do not want to face. We simply must walk forward—whether we like it or not. My family would have to find a way to go forward, and that way forward would include deep waters, rivers of difficulty, and the fires of oppression, as the prophet of God outlined in Isaiah 43.

> When you go through deep waters,
> I will be with you.
> When you go through rivers of difficulty,
> you will not drown.
> When you walk through the fire of oppression,
> you will not be burned up;
> the flames will not consume you.
> For I am the Lord, your God,
> the Holy One of Israel, your Savior. (Isaiah 43:2–3 NLT)

Do you question how a mere man could have written those words of encouragement with such confidence? I do. There's only one answer as to how he did it. *He had firsthand experience.* Firsthand experience always validates the speaker. By the time Isaiah wrote chapter 43, he had already been through deep waters, he had waded through rivers of difficulty, and he had been through the fires of oppression. Isaiah had a respectable career as a scribe in Jerusalem when God appear to him and called him to be a prophet. He prophesied for sixty years to his own nation saying that unless they repented and turned back to God they would be overthrown and taken into exile. It was a message that no one wanted to listen to or heed. Isaiah was unpopular, rejected, and eventually executed. During his many years of obeying God, he experienced for himself what God will do for his child. *God will be with you, you will not drown, you will not be burned up, and flames will not consume you.* In short, Isaiah had been there, done that. His words are a monument to his trust in God.

But tragedies are different; we haven't been there before so we don't know how to act. Tragedy is never on anyone's calendar. It is never convenient. It never asks for permission to invade our lives. There is no forewarning, no safety drill, no sirens blaring, and no chance to prepare. It simply happens at will.

Even if the townspeople, neighbors, and onlookers suspected *something* might happen in the Oscar Bode family, the tragedy was still a shock. Suspicions are just that—suspicions. Yet when suspicions become real life, they take on new meaning. Instead of *maybes* or *what-ifs*, they become action. And it is the action that strips us of the power to control our destinies, our hopes, and our dreams. It steals the very fiber of our security, well-being, and peace of mind from us and we are left vulnerable. Our emotions are volatile, unpredictable, and at times downright fickle. Our souls—mind, will, and emotions—have taken a direct hit. They are wounded and bleeding. The way we react to our wounds may be different for every person, but the damage is real.

*Tragedy is never on anyone's calendar. It is never convenient. It never asks for permission to invade our lives.*

In these critical times of life—when things are out of control—it is imperative to know where to turn for help. Do you and I know where to turn? Our children would likely say, "Call 911." That could be the right answer in some cases, but not always. Sometimes there is nothing any human being can do to help us. Yet I do know one person who got the answer right. He is the psalmist who penned Psalm 121. Read the powerful declaration found in verses 1–2.

I look up to the mountains and hills, longing for God's help.
But then I realize that our true help and protection
come only from the Lord,

our Creator who made the heavens and the earth. (Psalm 121:1–2 TPT)

Knowing where to turn is perhaps half of the battle, yet so many people look elsewhere first. We become workaholics. We hit the road, the bottle, and the drugs—anything to silence the noise. We want to stifle what we feel, make it go away, or sleep it off as if it were a bad dream. The problem with that approach is that we eventually have to wake up, sober up, step up, and deal with it.

## By Grace Alone

Except for God's grace, no one would survive the deadening effects of tragedy. But for grace alone! God's grace is a marvelous thing, and it does marvelous things. Personally, I need grace—great grace actually, and lots of it. Don't we all? Life on earth is difficult, and there are circumstances that scream for grace—divine influence upon the heart, as defined by *Strong's Concordance.* I am so grateful that it is available, abundant, and free. And when we know where to get it, it's ours for the asking.

When my granddaughter was six years old, she told me that she had found her name in her new Bible. "I found it three times," she declared as if I didn't believe her. I was a bit leery, not recalling Kalei in the Bible, but then I remembered that her middle name is Grace. I assured her that her name is indeed found many times in the Bible. According to Bible Gateway, the word *grace* appears in the Bible anywhere from ninety-five to 217 times, depending on the version. Here are some familiar favorites on grace:

- Noah found grace.[1]
- He gives us more grace.[2]
- By the grace of God, I am what I am.[3]
- From His fullness we have all received grace upon grace.[4]
- He who came from the Father was full of grace.[5]
- Great grace was upon them all.[6]
- Where sin abounded, grace did much more abound.[7]

- My grace is sufficient for you.[8]
- By grace you are saved, through faith … it is the gift of God.[9]
- That we may … find grace to help in time of need.[10]

God's Word is full of grace—and so is God. Grace has been described as God's unmerited favor—that which I don't deserve. In the words of her amazing hymn "He Giveth More Grace,"[11] Annie Johnson Flint captures the activity and availability of God's grace for us. According to Flint, God dishes out His grace more than we can grasp in our wildest imaginations, even when using the multiplication factor. But I do know this about His grace: it is the very substance I cannot live without. Simply put, I need it *desperately*.

In my own day-to-day living (or you could say where the rubber meets the road), obtaining God's great grace-gift operates something like this:

- I don't deserve that God would rescue me from my sinful self. *I breathe in a breath of grace.*
- I don't deserve that He would be patient with me who is so impatient. *I lean in closer to God and ask for more grace, please.*
- I don't deserve to be called His child when I don't act like one. *I gulp in yet another portion of grace.*
- I don't deserve to feel His love when I have been unlovable. *I breathe deeply, reaching for still more grace.*
- I don't deserve to be pardoned when I have judged another. *Now I'm gasping for grace upon grace—multiplied grace!*

And what does God do in response to my needs? He gives me grace over and over again, according to Flint's song. With every breath, grace fills the hollowness of this earthen vessel with God Himself. God and grace are intricately bound together, for when we find that we have grace, we will also find that we have God.

As we recognize and admit our neediness before God, we can gladly claim His grace for ourselves. God's grace is medicinal—healing to our wounded souls—and its benefits are vast.

> Grace soothes a weary soul with His presence.
> Grace calms nerves that are stretched to breaking.

Grace cradles faith that buckled underneath the load.
Grace sets feet upright that didn't stay on top of the water.
Grace refocuses on Him eyes that were once fixed on circumstances.
Grace strengthens weak knees and hands that hang down.
Grace renews a mind that is drained from ongoing attacks.
Grace refreshes a heart that fainted instead of praying.
Grace rekindles love for the One who never quits loving.
Grace holds up those who face tragedy when they think there is no way possible.

The four adult children of Oscar and Ethel Bode and their spouses would have to find their way through the maze of emotions, deep grief, and changed lives. Grace would be their mainstay.

## The Next Steps

Uncle Floy picked up the pieces of his own heart and began to put the pieces of tragedy aside. Once the news of the tragedy spread, Aunt Virginia opened their home to many relatives. There were things to be done almost immediately—caskets purchased, arrangements made, and funeral details set in place. Other things would take days, weeks, months, and maybe years to work through. It would be challenging and grueling all at the same time. Floy stepped up to the challenge.

Aunt Hallis and Uncle Carlos were the spiritual leaders in the family. Being the pastors of the local church, they were also leaders in their community. How they handled this tragedy and the crushing blow to their faith would be noticeable to hundreds of onlookers. Would they be strong enough to comfort others? Were they strong enough to allow weaker ones to lean on them? Would their faith hold up in this time of crisis? Oh yes, it did.

Buzzy told me his tenth birthday was just a few days after the funeral. He doesn't remember how she did it, but his mom made a birthday cake for him, just like any other normal birthday. Zane's birthday would follow a month later—and just as she and her mom had planned, she celebrated her birthday as well. This family would become a stabilizing force for the others. It has often been said that Hallis was the glue that held everything and everyone together. She continued to be that glue for her entire life.

My parents were living in California at the time of the tragedy, with my dad having been released from the US Army in 1945, exactly eight months before. When the news of the tragedy came, my mom went to take the call at the office of the apartment complex where they lived. While my dad waited in their apartment, a bird landed on the windowsill next to where he was sitting. An omen states that when a bird lands in a windowsill, it is a sign of bad news. Call it what you may, but it happened. Whether an omen or not, it gave my father a brief minute to brace himself for the worst news ever.

My dad thought through his predicament and how to handle getting his family back to Texas. He called his sister Hallis to tell her that they would be coming home to stay, knowing full well that home would never be the same. They were bringing all of their belongings in their car—clothes, a few household items, and my two-year-old brother who fit perfectly in the rumble seat. By design, they would not arrive in time for the funeral but a few days later.

My dad had been in combat while in Italy only months before and had seen more than his share of carnage. He told Hallis that he had helped stack the dead bodies of his friends onto trucks as if they were pieces of cardboard. He felt that he could not handle this triple funeral. The family understood. My cousins remembered Cecil, Della, and Ronnie pulling up to my aunt's house in their little car, which held everything they owned in this world.

LaVerne would have the most difficult time dealing with the tragedy of all the Bode children. She had, in fact, been Oscar's favorite, and her life was closely connected to the lives of her parents.

For my entire life, I have dealt with stomach issues—problems with indigestion, reflux, and sensitivity to coffee, spices, fried foods, etc. And for my entire life, I was told that I had a "Bode stomach." I was no different from my dad, siblings, aunts, uncles, and cousins. Because of the enormous stress the tragedy brought on LaVerne's life, she could digest only baby food for the next three to four years. Her recovery would not come quickly or easily, but it did come.

Once the funeral was behind them, these grown children had the task of determining what to do with their parents' belongings: a house, land, household goods, and livestock. Fortunately for them, some very thoughtful neighbors had cleaned up the kitchen. They had also cleverly covered up one bullet hole in the floor.

As far as household goods and furniture, the four couples met at their parents' home to divide their belongings. Taking one room at a time, the smaller items were put into four equal piles. The oldest got to choose first which pile he wanted on round one; the second oldest got to choose first on next round, and so forth. At last, the furniture was handled the same way, until all the belongings were divided. I clearly remember the bedroom furniture that my mom and dad slept on for many years. It was the bedroom furniture that had belonged to my grandparents.

The land, the house, the farm equipment, and the livestock were sold and the children received equal shares of the money. It had been divided fair and square. We do not know how their emotions served them on this day. We just know that they lived through it. My siblings and I were never taken to the home place of our grandparents. In fact, it was never mentioned.

For any of us to move toward healing, we must get beyond our past. Sounds simple enough, doesn't it? But it is not easy. Movement is required since it serves as part of the healing process. I consider it nothing short of a miracle that these eight souls handled this day at all. Even if they just *barely* handled it or *almost* handled it, it was still a miracle. They propelled themselves toward healing on this day. If I were to put myself in their shoes, I don't know if I could have survived it. But this I know: I would definitely have needed *grace* to do so.

Several years ago, I watched a young friend in her midthirties bury her husband and the father of their two young sons. He was a pastor of a growing church and their future looked bright and secure. That is, until Derrick *(not his real name)* learned that he had a fast-growing form of melanoma. Two years of fighting with everything they had, along with prayers for Derrick's healing being prayed around the world, did nothing to slow the ravaging disease.

Their story pierced my heart as it did thousands of other friends and church members. Yet there is one part of Cindy's story *(not her real name)* that I will never forget. Derrick's condition continued to deteriorate as the weeks went by. Her physical strength was all but gone. There seemed to be no answers and no hope. Death was imminent. In an email to her prayer support team, Cindy wrote, "I can't explain grace, but I am sure enjoying it."

For whatever life brings our way, even if it is tragic, God will not leave us without help. His amazing grace—abundant and free—will always be sufficient. It is always enough, it is always adequate, and God never gives it sparingly. In spite of every hard thing we face, God's grace will be there. That's what His Word promises to those who turn to Him.

There are many of us who can personally own these words of the psalmist: "You have allowed me to suffer much hardship, but you will restore me to life again and lift me up from the depths of the earth. You will restore me to even greater honor and comfort me once again" (Psalm 71:20-21 NLT).

> Hardly a life goes deep but has tragedy somewhere in it.[12]
> —Amy Carmichael

# CHAPTER SEVEN

# THE SURVIVORS

I have been a survivor on more than one occasion, as I am no stranger to death. I lost my mom to cancer when I was twenty-one years old, my dad to cancer when I was thirty-eight, and my husband and the father of my children to cancer when I was fifty-three. Cancer has taken more than its fair share, and I learned at an early age to hate the "C" word. It strips its victims of self-confidence, self-dependency, self-esteem, and lastly, self-worth. I've seen those with radiation wounds that burned more than intended, losses of hair and hope, and being left with a moon face and little resemblance to who they once were.

Cancer has no mercy. It is unyielding, unrelenting, and unfair. I have lived in close proximity to its devastation and seen firsthand its devilish greed to rob a victim of all the necessary pieces of life. It slowly disrobes one of everything, except perhaps for one's faith. Yes, faith. I've seen strong faith endure the cruel mockery of the voice that contends, "Where is your God now?" Eventually, a cancer victim is deprived of enough strength to carry on the fight and at last succumbs to the inevitable end, but still there is that faith—a faith that held strong and carried them safely to the Father's arms.

Yet each time I was forced to face the wiles of cancer, I survived. Though I'm not sure just how I managed to do that at the tender age of twenty-one. My immaturity and lack of faith didn't serve me well, and I made mistakes. Because I had a new baby to care for while my husband was away in military training, I basically put my life in neutral and thought I'd deal with it later. Nothing or no one I had come across in life up to that time had prepared me for my mom's death—nothing. But still I survived.

Seventeen years later, I would give up my dad. Because he had lived longer than my mom, it somehow seemed easier to endure. But the most likely reason would be that I was now more mature and had developed a stronger faith in God. Yet another fifteen years beyond the loss of my dad, I faced what I thought

*God was there. He was not ever not there!*

would never happen to me, since statistics were in my favor. At that time, the ratio of Americans who would develop cancer sometime in their life was one in four. Counting the four of us, this would now be three in four. Unthinkable!

My husband was diagnosed with full-blown, off-the-chart prostate cancer. We faced two years of hyperaggressive treatment for a hyperaggressive disease, including MD Anderson Cancer Hospital in Houston, Texas, and Oasis of Hope Cancer Hospital in Tijuana, Mexico. Yet two years to the day of the original diagnosis, he was gone from our lives. Being widowed at fifty-three was a shock to my life. There would be many difficult days ahead. I would scream, "Why?" at the top of my lungs and declare to God that I wanted my life back. But through it all, I could never say that nothing or no one had prepared me for this moment—because God had. He had brought me through the trials of loss not just once but twice. My faith had grown and matured, and while I thought on many occasions that I would surely drown, God threw me a lifeline.

*God was there. He was not ever not there!*

I learned by experience that surviving is hard. You learn to protect yourself from unnecessary pain, simply because there is enough necessary pain to cripple the best of us unless we learn to manage the sheer volume of it. And knowing what I now know, when I consider the tragedy that my family members were called upon to endure, I crater under the heaviness of what those early days and nights must have felt like to them. There were days when I thought I couldn't breathe because of my sorrow. Stale, heavy air lodged in my throat. It felt as though I were walking through a bad dream, but the dream never ended. Yet I cannot accurately compare my loss with what they endured. I didn't have visions of carnage to sort through, or recollection of subtle signs that were perhaps clues that may have prevented it all. I didn't have sorrow piled upon sorrow because of multiple deaths all at the same time. But what I did have was the very thing my family members had as well: *trust in a faithful God.*

> Not once did I walk alone—and neither did they.
> Not once did I drown in my sorrow—and neither did they.
> Not once did I feel so lost that I couldn't find my way—and neither did they.
> Not once did I believe God didn't care about my pain—and neither did they.
> Not once did I blame God for what had happened—and neither did they.
> Not once did I think the sun wouldn't come up in the morning—and neither did they.

You may ask, "How are you so sure you know these things about your family?" I know beyond a shadow of a doubt because my family actually survived. The newspapers that reported this tragedy back in 1946 were correct: they were survivors. All of them!

Despite the pain, the dreadful images, and the what-ifs, my family found the resilience and wherewithal to move on, even if their early steps were small. You see, they were who they were because of deep family roots. They had come from a long line of survivors of hard and difficult times, survivors of wars and battles,

*They were survivors because that is what survivors do—they survive.*

survivors of six weeks afloat on the Atlantic, survivors of enemy attacks, survivors of religious persecution, and survivors of tragedies. They were survivors because that is what survivors do—*they survive.*

## Looking for Answers

We are always looking for answers. As Christians, the place we turn for answers every time is to our God. Throughout life's lessons, we slowly learn that apart from Him, there are no answers. None. It is God and God alone who holds the key to the storehouse of all our needs: love, grace, mercy, help, healing, and hope. And when those needs are met by a loving Heavenly Father, we become survivors. We survive in a fallen, broken world because He enables us to do so. Missionary Amy Carmichael reminds us, "Remember that there is nothing you are asked to do in your own strength. Not the least thing, nor the greatest."[1]

It is important to both recognize and acknowledge that we have no strength of our own. The prophet Habakkuk was also looking for answers. His urgent cry to God rang out through his writings. "How long, O Lord, must I call for help? But you do not listen!" (Habakkuk 1:2 NLT). Habakkuk needed to hear from the God he trusted in order to have enough strength to face his current circumstances. Sound familiar? He also gave us a glimpse of how things turned out for those who trusted in themselves. "But they are deeply guilty, for their own strength is their god" (Habakkuk 1:11 NLT).

The Old Testament prophet had deep faith in a God who had proven Himself before. In spite of hardships, tragedy, destruction, and violence all around him, Habakkuk wrote these stirring words of encouragement to others and as a testimony of his faith in a caring God. He declared that he would rejoice in the Lord in spite of what appeared to be hopeless circumstances.

> Even though the fig trees have no blossoms,
> and there are no grapes on the vines;
> even though the olive crop fails,
> and the fields lie empty and barren;
> even though the flocks die in the fields,
> and the cattle barns are empty,
> yet I will rejoice in the Lord!
> I will be joyful in the God of my salvation! (Habakkuk 3:17–18 NLT)

I think modern-day Christianity is too lacking in miracles, while Jesus's day was filled with such phenomenon. But I wonder just what it is that brings the most glory to God: an instant, one-time deliverance from that thing that threatens to make us fall or a faithful Presence that comes to our rescue over and over to provide the strength we need to resist the threatening thing yet another time?

## Learning to Walk—Again

I believe it is the day by day walking forward—placing one foot out in front of the other to claim victory long before we reach our goal—that glorifies our faithful God the most. Is it not in the rescue from a near fall that His child gradually develops strong spiritual muscles? Are we not His little ones learning to walk again?

I resigned from my corporate job just in time to watch my one-year-old grandson learn to walk. It was a delight to watch as he struggled to keep his balance on his chubby, little legs. One day while babysitting him, I picked up my pen and wrote how his real-time struggle closely mirrored my attempts to walk with God. I believe God watches us with the same delight as I had watched my grandson.

### Learning to Walk

Precious little feet learning to walk,
Still just a baby, can't even talk.
So much like us walking with God,
Some ups and downs on the path we trod.

To where he's going, he no longer crawls.
He'll chance walking even if he falls.
Chubby little legs he's learning to use,
Yet there'll be times, his balance lose.

Holding to things so he feels safe,
And just like us, it'll take some faith.
Parents close by to urge him on,
Holding his hand 'til fear is gone.

He carefully measures to see how far
It is from him to where you are.
You bid him come, in you he'll trust.
Turning loose of things is always a must.

He misses the mark, you soothe the pain,
Set him upright, and say, "Try again."
Each step is important, failure is risked,
But a step not taken is learning missed.

Building confidence 'til the battle's won,
For he must walk before he can run.
So much like us and the Father above
Learning to walk in His great love.

Learning to walk in the natural is basically mastering how to keep one's balance. It takes practice and lots of it. When tragedy invades our lives, we are thrown off-balance, and regaining our balance speaks to our deepest need after losing a loved one. It is as if the bearings—where we are and where other things are—have shifted.[2] Who we once were is now different, like not being a wife or not being a part of a couple after my husband died. Where we thought we were going has been rerouted. Some things we planned to do are no longer possible. So much has changed that we are shaky at best, and to regain our balance is no easy feat. Yet in order to keep walking forward, we must regain our balance.

"The way you keep walking?" writes Ann Voskamp. "You may be wounded. You may be hurting. You may be limping. You may feel alone and overwhelmed and an unspoken broken—but you're no victim. You're not just a survivor. You're a thriver. You may bleed—but you rise."[3]

The women in my family, whom I adored while growing up, were strong, molded, and carefully crafted daughters of the same God I serve today. The aunt who never uttered an unkind word about anyone didn't gain that quality overnight. And the aunt with the sweetest voice I'd ever heard didn't get that way because of a one-time, instant deliverance. My aunt who thought hard work was how one is supposed to live came by it the hard way. And my mom, who had the rare qualities of graciousness and a super attitude, didn't simply wish upon a star one night.

The men from my childhood had also been shaped by their Creator. My uncle, who was known for his giving, helping, serving, and saving others from fires, had come through some fires of his own. My dad, who loved quietness, found strength in God when there were no words. "In quietness and confidence is your strength," the prophet Isaiah told us in Isaiah 30:15 (NLT). My terror-on-wheels uncle was called into the ministry, and as a pastor, he would spend his life standing at the side of countless grieving friends and neighbors, helping them find their own way through sorrow.

The song "God Leads Us Along," written by G. A. Young in 1903, describes the mayhem of life on earth so well. This songwriter got it right.

> Some through the waters, some through the flood
> Some through the fire, but all through the blood
> Some through great sorrow, but God gives a song
> In the night season and all the day long.[4]

The key word is *through*—*through* waters; *through* floods; *through* fire; *through* blood! The saints of old listed in the Heroes of Faith in Hebrews 11 came *through!* My aunts and uncles came *through!* My parents came *through!* The grandchildren who were onlookers to their parents suffering came *through!* And so did I. We all came *through!* Every. Last. One. Of. Us!

Each of us can testify that in the greatest hour of trial, God does indeed give a song. He gives it not just in that dark night of sorrow but also all the days of our lives if we cling to Him and keep on clinging to Him. He is a faithful Presence that comes to our rescue over and over to give us strength to keep moving forward.

After two years of struggle with my sorrow, I came out on the other side—knowing full well that it was God who had rescued me time and again. The Twenty-Third Psalm had been an anchor during my healing process. In the quiet early hours one morning, I expanded it. Sometimes we need to expand things: our faith, our hope, our sight, and our confidence in God. And all the while they are actually expanding us—who we are, how we think, how we love, and how we trust. That is what I did in my paraphrased version of the Twenty-Third Psalm based on the New Living Translation. (The italicized words are from the psalm, and my own words are not italicized.)

## My Expansion of the Twenty-Third Psalm

*The Lord is my shepherd; I have all that I need* just because He is.
    *He lets me rest in green meadows,* even when the world
        is spinning around me at tremendous speed.
*He leads me beside peaceful streams,* though at times it seems like
    rushing waters that will soon overtake me and I will drown.
        *He renews my strength,* even if I think that I cannot go on
another day, another mile. He is restoring my health, my mind,
    and my well-being, although I feel sick in body and soul.
*He guides me along right paths, bringing honor to His name.* His pathways
    lead me to people and places that are good for me and bring healing
        to my life. I can be confident that the paths He has chosen for me
        are the right ones for they are paths of faith, trust, and courage.
*Even when I walk through the darkest valley, I will not be afraid* of all the
    devastation it brings to my life. I can do this *for you are close by me.*
I know that you will bring me out of that valley safely because *your rod*
*and your staff protect and comfort me* from all that can harm me there.
    *You prepare a feast for me in the presence of my enemies*—in
        the very place where the enemy is trying to destroy my faith,
            and yes, my very life. There I can find nourishment.
You welcome me to your table and *you honor me by anointing my head*
*with oil* of comfort, the Holy Spirit. This precious oil runs down over
    my life and covers it with a soothing ointment of peace and grace.
        *My cup overflows with blessings* because of your great
            graciousness to me. I have so much to be thankful for.
*Surely your goodness and unfailing love will pursue me all the days of my*
*life,* because you have given me your promise to do so. And someday
    I will go to be with my shepherd and my loved ones who have gone
        there before me, *and I will live in the house of the Lord forever.*

My expansion of the Twenty-Third Psalm meant much to me in the midst of my return to wholeness. It assured me of God's care during my days of sorrow and struggle, but it also helped me look forward to a time when sorrow and struggle would go away. You may feel like that isn't possible for you—that such deep sorrow will ever go away. Rest assured, dear one, that it will. God's promises are true, and His unfailing love will see to it that better days are ahead for all who mourn.

Consider yourself a thriver.

Consider yourself a survivor now.

Consider yourself coming through this trial and out on the other side.

Out of the wreck I rise.[5] —Robert Browning

CHAPTER EIGHT

———

# THE PURPOSE

In 2002, Pastor Rick Warren released his best-selling book, *The Purpose Driven Life,* in which he outlines God's five purposes for human life on earth. By 2007, 30 million copies had been sold. It was on the *New York Times* Best Sellers List for over ninety weeks, and more than 50 million copies have been sold in more than 137 languages.

I received my first copy of the book as a gift from my son two weeks after my husband slipped from this life, leaving me alone in the world. It was as if I needed a user's manual for the new life I was facing. The title alone enticed me to start reading as soon as it was in my hands.

In the early pages of the book, Rick Warren wrote amazing words of wisdom.

> You cannot arrive at your life's purpose by starting with a focus on yourself. You must begin with God, your Creator. You exist only because God wills that you exist. You were made by God and for God—and until you understand that, life will never make sense. It's only in God that we discover our origin, our identity, our meaning, our purpose, our significance, and our destiny. Every other path leads to a dead end.[1]

My husband and I had been together since I was sixteen years old and were married ten days before my eighteenth birthday. Everything we had done in building our lives, we had done together. For thirty-six years, my marriage and family had been my purpose for existing. Suddenly that was gone, and nothing made sense—not my identity, purpose, significance, and definitely not my destiny. The truth is that I didn't

*The focus is not on why God let this happen but on what we do now that it has happened.*

even know the right place to start to figure it all out. I naturally thought it would have been to focus on myself, but according to Rick Warren, apparently not.

So how do we make sense of it all—if one ever can? How can we know the purpose for any given thing, or for any one of us? How can we possibly know the purpose in a tragedy—if there is one? Apparently, a lot of people—perhaps as many as 50 million of us—are looking for the *purpose* in our circumstances. I certainly was when I devoured Warren's book.

If there is one thing we know about tragedy, it is that tragedies don't come with an explanation. Since there is no explanation, the focus is not on why God let this happen but on what we do *now* that it has happened.

I recently met with a beautiful, young friend and mother of three small children who had been shocked by her husband's words. "I want a divorce." His cutting words had sliced through her heart. Her countenance revealed the pain as she shared what had gone wrong in their marriage over the past year. I came prepared and handed her a small, framed, word picture that had been setting on my desk for several years. It was the scripture found in Isaiah 26:3. I had changed the pronouns in the verse to read "she" rather than "he" in an effort to make it a personalized message to me from my Heavenly Father. It was a verse that had held me steady during troubling times in my own life—a time when I had greatly needed peace.

You will keep her in perfect peace whose mind is stayed on You, because she trusts in You. (Isaiah 26:3 NJKV; modified by author)

She stared at it, silently processing the words. With a deep yearning in her voice, she looked up at me and asked, "How do you do that?"

One simple, gut-honest question: how do you keep your mind on God when all havoc is breaking loose in your life?

Isn't that what we need to know most? How do we do that? How do we get up the morning after the funeral, the words asking for divorce, the phone call saying our child has been in a car wreck, or learning that drugs have once again sabotaged a family member—you know, the chaos that just invaded our world? How do we keep putting one foot in front of the other?

Jesus never chides us for asking the how-to questions. That is what He is actually waiting for us to do—*ask*. He loves to meet us right smack-dab in the middle of not knowing what to do next. Our biggest problem is for whatever reason, we are afraid to ask.

Never once has Jesus been disappointed that we don't have our tragedy all figured out. I am reminded of the lyrics of a song by Matt Redman, "Never Once,"[2] that speak of being on a mountain and looking back over our past. We can all do that—seeing, feeling, and knowing that with every difficult step we made throughout our lives, God was there with us. Matt's amazing lyrics tell of battlefields, struggles, wounds, and the scars that visibly mark our trail. And for the scars we can't see, we have the inward, gut-wrenching memories that sure feel like scars. We can all relate to the tough times, the excruciating circumstances, and trials of life that God was always with us.

Dear reader, rejoice! It is true. Never once has God failed to keep His word to His children. The writer of 1 Kings 8:56 states it clearly. "There has not failed one word of all His good promises, which he promised through his servant Moses." So why do we feel that God has failed us now—here on this present battleground?

I suspect that we've all been here—on this battleground or any battleground for that matter. Battlegrounds come in many sizes, shapes, and colors. These include the dreaded "D" words of divorce, disease, depression, death, dementia, drowning, divided hearts, double minds, and double jeopardy. But isn't that what life is made of?

## Is God Really Good All the Time?

When my husband lost his battle with cancer at the age of fifty-five, I coined a new phrase. "Life is hard, and then you die." Obviously, I was grappling with God over my loss. It happened about the same time the Don Moen song "God Is Good All the Time" became popular in churches. Everywhere I turned, I heard this feel-good song that leads one to believe that it is true. The problem was it wasn't true for me. Not now anyway.

I was met head-on with the same question that my young friend had asked. "How do you do that?" How do I believe God is good all the time? I also needed to know why all the Christians were singing, "God is good all the time," when my painful experience had proven otherwise.

Ann Voskamp writes, "I'd heard preached what Jesus never had—some *pseudo-good news* that if you just pray well, sing well, worship well, live well, and give lots, well, you get to take home a mind and body that are well."[3] My husband and I had done all those things—and done them well. So then why didn't it turn out well for me?

My sons said goodbye to a father they needed at the ages of thirty-two and twenty-nine. They were starting their families and careers, buying land, building houses, making dreams, and planning futures. The morning that my husband died, my five-year-old grandson begged to talk to his pawpaw one more time because there was something he needed to tell him. And then there was me. I was launched into the unknown territory of life as a widow—with a broken heart, broken dreams, and a near-broken faith.

I fear we've all heard preached much hype about nothing that soothes for the moment yet has little impact on the real issues of life—those times when our lives come crashing down. For me, at this juncture, the journey to discover how to keep my mind on God and gain that peace He offered me was a long one.

I totally get Ann Voskamp's summary of that cliché. "*God is good* is not a stale one-liner when all's happy, but a saving lifeline when all's bad."[4] It took years before I finally figured out that God's goodness is not gauged by the things He does for us. Instead, His goodness is a fact! God is good because it is His nature to be good. Nothing and no one can alter that truth. Since God *is* good, then it is also true that God *is* good all the time, at any time, and every time—whether it be at our happiest moment in life or in the face of tragedy. And that saving, lifeline truth is worth grasping hold of, and yes, it is worth singing about.

If God is good all the time, then bad things that happen to us cannot be a result of God being *not* good. Since that isn't possible, then what could possibly be the reason or purpose for the hard things we face?

The wise writer of Proverbs 27:17 tells us that "iron sharpens iron." Quite honestly, that sounds cold and hard to me, and I much prefer warm and fuzzy. Yet the very hardness of iron is what qualifies it to sharpen other iron—to rub against it and make a difference. This sharpening happens because of the closeness, the friction, and the impact, and that is what makes it better and more efficient. The remainder of the verse says "so a man sharpens the countenance of his friend."

We hear a similar concept in 2 Corinthians 1:4 (NLT) when the apostle Paul wrote, "He (God) comforts us *in all our troubles* so that we can comfort others. When they are troubled, we will be able to give them the same comfort God has given us." In short, God helps us in times of trouble, so we can help another person in trouble.

It's no surprise to any of us that God's ways are higher than ours. His plans are always bigger. They are always more noble, more moral, more upright, and certainly more merciful. He cares about us, but He also cares about others. Ultimately, God's plan is to rescue every person on planet earth. And right at the heart of His great plan, He has inserted us—His children. We are called to be like Him, think like Him, love like Him, forgive like Him, and reach like Him.

As our journey with God starts to shape us and sharpen us for God's purpose, we gradually come to learn that it's not about *us;* it's about saving a lost world. God's plan to grow us

*If God is good all the time, then bad things that happen to us cannot be a result of God being not good.*

up and help us accept our calling is so we can reach for something bigger than *ourselves*. God desires mature sons and daughters who have moved from being needy baby Christians to those who can give out of their reservoir of life experiences to meet the needs of others.

In his stirring book *The Return of the Prodigal Son*,[5] Henri J. M. Nouwen perfectly defines the three spiritual conditions in which we can find ourselves. The first is the lost and wayward son—the prodigal—who thought only of himself and his own pleasure. Some of us fit here. We're wasteful with our lives, our resources, and our love. We make reckless choices, paying little attention to whom they may hurt. Our selfish and excessive ways earn us the title of being the *lost* son or daughter where our fleshly desires have separated us from our Father's house—yet never from our Father's love.

The second condition in which we could find ourselves is that of the older, embittered son. He had stayed at home and obeyed his father, yet he held much contempt for his younger brother. He couldn't even find the decency within his heart to be happy that his once *lost* brother had been found. It was selfishness hidden behind his title of being the obedient one. You know, the righteous one who never did anything wrong, never left home, never got a tattoo, and never looked *lost*. Today, our churches are filled with these sons and daughters who find it hard to move over and share a pew with the *once lost* sons of our Father.

And then there is the third spiritual condition that was noticeably revealed in the aged father. After years of suffering from the selfish behavior of his two sons, he had from that hard place matured and grown to become like the Heavenly Father Himself. We see in his character that he was truly a giver of grace, mercy, forgiveness, and unquestionably extravagant love. Nouwen writes, "He loves us with a first love, an unlimited, unconditional love, wants us to be his beloved children, and tells us to become as loving as himself."[6]

## Shaped for a Reason

What does God shaping us have to do with our pain? The answer is much! Our pain has much to do with God shaping us to be usable in His kingdom. Our kingdom calling is to rescue our next-door neighbor, the person who carries out our groceries (if anyone does that anymore), or the person serving our Starbucks latte at the drive-through window. *It requires hard iron on hard hearts to make an impact on hard issues.* How else is God going to make us hard against the blows of life lest He sharpens us with hard things? And if He doesn't sharpen us, how can He use us?

"We can take comfort that God is behind our trials. He does not train those whom He does not intend to use in wonderful ways,"[7] wrote Chris Tiegreen.

God intricately shapes and prunes the lives of those He intends to use. I think it is interesting that we pray and ask the Lord to use us in His kingdom's work on earth, yet when He does, we complain about feeling "used" by others. But we can't have it both ways. Either we want to be used by God or we don't. And if we choose to be used, it will always cost us something.

It is basically *our calling* that triggers our need of hard places and hard things. Until we grow up and grasp the bigger, higher plan of God for our lives, we will continue to resist every hard thing that comes our way. In James 1:2, we're told to "count it all joy when you fall into various trials," and we wonder what in the world James is talking about. We also hear Paul say, "Therefore I take pleasure in infirmities, in reproaches, in needs, in persecutions, in distresses, for Christ's sake. For when I am weak, then I am strong" (2 Corinthians 12:10).

Because God is always seeking the lost, reaching for them, and trying to gain their attention, He needs you and me to engage in that same heavenly cause. It is within that framework that we can at least begin to understand our purpose on earth and why God allows hard things to happen in our world. It's all about eternity. It's all about getting the Good News to lost and dying people. *Our Daily Bread* author Dave Branon wrote, "God's good news is too good to keep to ourselves." It's all about growing us up and conforming us into the image of Jesus. It's never been about anything else.

Rick Warren wrote, "Jesus taught that spiritual maturity is never an end in itself. Maturity is for ministry! We grow up in order to give out."[8] If that's the case, then our hard places are our opportunities to do the giving out. They actually do have a purpose—a purpose that is aligned with God's greater plan. But we may ask, "Why would hard places be opportunities?" That's a bit optimistic, don't you think? The answer is simple. They are opportunities because the lost world is watching us. The lost world does not know where to turn (or they wouldn't still be lost) or who to call when tragedy strikes. As God's children, we do know where to turn, and we do know who to call in desperate times. We should be able to look back on our lives and say, "God, I thank You for every hard place You used to bring me here."

Now we know *how* God sharpens us and *why* He sharpens us. A great example is that of the young, favorite-son Joseph who could easily recall the pain of being sold into slavery by his jealous brothers. Yet many years later, it was the trained-in-the-school-of-hard-knocks Joseph who told his fearful brothers, "But as for you, you meant evil against me; but God meant it for good, in order to bring it about as it is this day, to save many people alive" (Genesis 50:20).

## Not for the Fainthearted

Desiring maturity or nobility without expecting to pay a price for it is somewhat like a young man entering a US Army Recruiting Office and announcing that he wants to join the army. What he really wants is to sign up for the uniform and the title—and some rank would be nice too—but he doesn't actually want to train or fight. He mostly wants the appearance of belonging to the unit. Can't you hear some tough staff sergeant clue him in on what it means to serve your country?

I sometimes think we have similar *wannabes* in the modern-day church. Some people want to have the title of Christian, wear the uniform of being good and caring, be a part of the unit especially if they're running for any office, but they don't really want to go into training, and they certainly don't want to serve.

Perhaps the American dream has messed up our thinking. We are programmed from early childhood to believe that the only good life is a long life, a prosperous one, filled with excitement, entertainment, and success—and of course, without any cost to us. When anything alters that myth, we think we've been shortchanged.

But that's not true, according to Rick Warren. "What matters is not the duration of your life, but the *donation* of it. Not how long you lived, but how you lived."[9] Jesus actually said it even plainer than Rick Warren. "If you try to hang on to your life, you will lose it. But if you give up your life for my sake and for the sake of the Good News, you will save it" (Mark 8:35 NLT).

All of us long to have a life of meaning and purpose. That's the goal we reach for, whether it is a short life or a long one. That rings true in the short life of Rachel Scott, the first victim of the Columbine High School shooting on April 20, 1999. Along with eleven other students and one teacher, seventeen-year-old Rachel had her life cut short for seemingly no reason. Yet more than twenty years later, her father, Darrell Scott, is still a crusader for addressing the issue of ongoing school violence. In a meeting with President Trump, he said, "We need to create a culture of connectedness in our schools to help prevent mass killings."[10] He is also not afraid to tackle the hard issues of mental illness.

In attempting to get our minds around any logical purpose for such a horrific event, it is necessary that we look beyond the tragedy to Rachel's new life in heaven. Rev. Porter made this statement at her memorial service: "You have graduated early from this life to a far better one, where there is no sorrow, violence, or death."[11]

While death may seem final to us, it is not. In Gloria Gaither's book titled *Heaven,* she wrote, "You never lose someone when you know where to find them."[12] Knowing where our loved ones are is perhaps the only condolence that soothes our pain. Having some grand purpose to connect to our tragedy doesn't make it any less gut-wrenching and cause us to say, "Oh sure, now I understand what God was doing." We simply cannot get there. And when no matter how hard we try we cannot connect tragedy to a divine purpose, we are left with only one thing to do: leave it in the hands of a just God. That is what Jesus did.

> For God called you to do good even if it means suffering, just as Christ suffered for you. He is your example, and you must follow in his steps. He never sinned, nor ever deceived anyone. He did not retaliate when he was insulted, nor threaten revenge when he suffered. He left his case in the hands of God, who always judges fairly. (1 Peter 2:21–23 NLT)

> God is not concerned about our plans; He doesn't ask, "Do you want to go through this loss of a loved one, this difficulty, or this defeat?" No, He allows these things for His own purpose. The things we are going through are

either making us sweeter, better, and nobler men and women, or they are making us more critical and fault-finding, and more insistent on our own way.[13] —Oswald Chambers

We are not called upon to understand why God does what He does, but we are called upon to trust His great wisdom and love, even in the most devastating of circumstances. After all, this is not a walk of understanding but a walk of faith. Our purpose here is to offer ourselves to Him for His divine purpose. It matters not whether He chooses to use us in good times or in bad times. Both are designed by God so He might tell His story through our lives.

God is continually involved in our redemption. He is in the business of an ongoing redemption in the life of each Christian, continually taking the bad and using it for good—if released to Him for that purpose.[14] —Miriam Huffman Rockness

# CHAPTER NINE

---

# THE WOUNDS

I was curious as to what the Greek definition for the word *wounds* might be, since I clearly felt wounded after my husband's death. I was actually surprised to learn that it comes from the root word *trauma*. Trauma is a word that we are quite familiar with in our modern-day culture, as we have trauma centers for those who experience bodily catastrophes and require urgent care. I was also surprised that *Webster's Dictionary* gives an even broader definition of *trauma*, which better defines what anyone who has lost loved ones might deal with. *Webster's* says trauma is "a bodily injury, wound or shock; a painful emotional experience or shock often producing a lasting psychic effect and sometimes a neurosis (mental functional disorder characterized by anxiety, compulsion, phobia, depression, or disassociation)."

While I did not sustain any bodily injury from my ordeal, I certainly sustained injury to my soul, which is made up of my mind, will, and emotions. In some sense, I felt traumatized. I had at times over three to four years experienced anxiety, depression, and disassociation. Thankfully, none of them were lasting. Whether these terms properly described the side effects of the loss of a loved one or not, I was left with what certainly seemed like wounds—not visible bodily wounds yet wounds nonetheless. To deny that they are wounds serves no purpose. I believe that the fastest path to healing for any kind of wound is to recognize it, admit it, and seek out the Healer of all wounds.

If there had been trauma centers back in 1946, my family would have been prime candidates for whatever trauma centers offer—be it physical, mental, or emotional. Physical injuries often get immediate attention, while mental and emotional ones are pushed back into our souls and expected to wait until a more convenient time. The problem with that line of thinking is that often they are just as pressing for urgent care as anything else. Stuffing things inside indefinitely can be disastrous to our overall well-being. I think stuffing is most likely the cause of some behaviors we see today. A sufferer of mental anguish has stuffed things far too long, and eventually it erupts within him or her. The eruption of their pain is carried out in mass shootings and other acts of violence against society.

It could be that no person actually sees our mental and emotional needs, except for our Heavenly Father—if we are good at pretending those needs don't exist. But God sees and knows our deepest hurts, and He cares deeply. In the book of Luke, we find an excellent word picture for how our Lord Jesus tends to our wounds.

> Jesus replied with a story: "A Jewish man was traveling from Jerusalem down to Jericho, and he was attacked by bandits. They stripped him of his clothes, beat him up, and left him half dead beside the road.
>
> "By chance a priest came along. But when he saw the man lying there, he crossed to the other side of the road and passed him by. A Temple assistant walked over and looked at him lying there, but he also passed by on the other side.
>
> "Then a despised Samaritan came along, and when he saw the man, he felt compassion for him. Going over to him, the Samaritan soothed his wounds with olive oil and wine and bandaged them. Then he put the man on his own donkey and took him to an inn, where he took care of him. The next day he handed the innkeeper two silver coins, telling him, 'Take care of this man. If his bill runs higher than this, I'll pay you the next time I'm here.'" (Luke 10:30–35 NLT)

Several things happened in this story that are worthy of mention. It is helpful to see Jesus as the Good Samaritan and ourselves in the place of the injured man. First we realize that Jesus *saw* the wounded man and had compassion on him. How very important that we who have been wounded know that Jesus *sees* our wounds and has compassion on us as well. Secondly, Jesus went to him, just as Jesus comes to us at our point of need. Next Jesus bandaged the man's wounds, pouring oil and wine on them and wrapping them tightly. The reference to oil in the Bible is the Holy Spirit (the Comforter), and the wine represents the blood of Jesus— the cleansing, atoning, and redeeming blood. What better medicine could we ask for than that? Jesus wraps us in His Spirit and applies His atoning blood to our wounds.

Take note in the story that Jesus bandaged the wounds *before* He moved the victim. At first, we may feel too traumatized to be moved or to deal with our wounds. It is simply enough just to get through the next day or the next event. Jesus holds us close during those times until we are ready to move on. The oil and the wine were considered medicine in Jesus's day. He didn't just wrap up those wounds. He poured medication on them. He wanted them to heal, not just be covered up. So it is with our wounds. If we try to hide them, they won't heal, and if they do begin to heal, it will take longer and leave deeper scars. We must have the proper medication of oil and wine to heal properly.

Next Jesus carried the wounded man to a place of restoration, and that is what Jesus wants to do for us. That place may at home today and away from home tomorrow or next week, but it will be a place away from the world where we can mend both physically and mentally. It will also be a place where we can be nurtured spiritually. In that place of restoration, Jesus will care for us. He will be our Caregiver. Furthermore, He will stay as long as we need Him to stay.

Then Jesus made arrangements for someone else to care for the wounded man, perhaps what we might call short-term care. God will send people into our lives as support people—family members, friends, church family, etc. Support groups are so valuable to us. They are there when we can't go it alone. We must be careful to allow those God brings to us to actually help us. There is no value in trying to go it alone when we're not ready.

Next instructions are given for the wounded's long-term care. A modern-day translation of the Good Samaritan's promise might sound like this: "Whatever you need and whatever it takes for you to get better, I'll pay for it. I've got you covered. Nothing is too much!"

When we can see it this way, the words of Psalm 147:3 (NLT) will make complete sense to us. "He heals the brokenhearted and bandages their wounds." Read that again. Jesus is a loving and kind caregiver. He knows our pain, our fears, and our insecurities during this recovery time. As always, He is watching over His children with compassion. After all, a loss is a loss, and a wound is a wound. No matter how a wound is inflicted upon us, it is painful and cannot be ignored. It must be dealt with, and it must be healed. God has made full provision for our wounds to heal.

*He is always using our trials to bring us closer to Himself and more useful to His kingdom.*

During my own personal struggle, I often felt as though what I believed about healing didn't match what I experienced. Our preconceived ideas can lead us astray, and many times I had to go back to square one and ask the Lord to show me clearly what He was trying to teach me. I do know that any mismatch between what His Word says and how I understand it is my problem and not His—because God cannot lie.

One example of this mismatch occurred when I claimed and believed a verse of scripture found in Psalm 118:17 that my husband would live and not die. When he died, I was both disappointed and confused. Following his death, I struggled with the mismatch of reality and what I considered a promise of God that he would not die. My peace didn't come overnight but took months to process and accept what had *actually* happened to my husband. His body had died (a reality), yet he was still living (another reality). He simply made a change in residence—from earth to heaven. Eternal life begins when we accept Jesus as our Lord and Savior, and it never ends. Oh, our place of residence can change, but that eternal life of God within us will live on forever.

God always has a higher purpose for our trials—and yes, even our wounds—than what we can see from our human perspective. He has truth to reveal to us, just like the example about eternal life, and He never wastes any situation or any circumstance to do so. He is always using our trials to bring us closer to Himself and more useful to His kingdom.

In God's efforts to conform us to the image of His Son, we must *learn* His ways since they are higher than our ways. In Psalm 119:71, the psalmist wrote these words: "It is good for me that I have been afflicted, that I may *learn* your statutes."

While we prefer not to believe so, God does have a purpose in our suffering. Yet this idea is in stark contrast to much of the hypergrace teaching we hear today. But simply stated, it is good for us. The truth is that we will not learn His ways any other way. With that in mind, I began to explore all the things that I had experienced and tried to determine what good or benefit had come out of them. I penned what I called "Why the Wounds?"

## Why the Wounds?

Unless I had been wounded, I would not
    know the One who binds up wounds.
Unless I had been brokenhearted, I would not
    know the Healer of broken hearts.
Unless I had cried bitter tears, I would not
    know Him who wipes away all tears.
Unless I had felt pain, I would not know the
    One with healing in His wings.
Unless I had been discomforted, I would
    not know the Comforter.
Unless I had loved and lost, I would not
    know the Lover of my soul.
Unless I had been downcast, I would not know
    the One who lifts up of my head.
Unless I had been lonely, I would not know the
    Friend who sticks closer than a brother.
Unless I had been abandoned, I would not
    know the Father to the fatherless.
Unless I had been needy, I would not
    know the Supplier of every need.

Unless I had endured great loss, I would
    not know the Restorer of life.
Unless I had gone astray, I would not
    know the Good Shepherd.
Unless I had failed, I would not know
    the Son of Righteousness.
Unless I had been in bondage, I would
    not know the Redeemer.
Unless I had been hopeless, I would
    not know the God of hope.
Unless I had been sorrowful, I would
    not know the Joy-giver.
Unless I had been without peace, I would
    not know the Prince of Peace.
Unless I had been helpless, I would not know
    the power of His resurrection.
Unless I had suffered, I would not know
    the fellowship of His suffering.
Unless I had been tested, I would not know
    that great is His faithfulness.
Unless I had been weak, I would not know
    that His grace is sufficient for me.
Unless I had been lost, I would not know the Savior.
For out of the anguish of the soul, revelation is birthed.

The question for us right here in this place of suffering is to ask ourselves, "Have I ever used my pain to climb to a higher place in God?" It is in this place of piercing pain that I came to understand that out of the anguish of our souls, revelation is birthed (comes to life). Each blow that God had allowed in my life opened for me a newer and deeper revelation of God's greatness and goodness. In each of the places listed above, the end result is a higher plane than where we once were. If that is true, and it is, then we too can indeed say with the psalmist, "It is good for me that I have been afflicted."

In Hebrews 5:8 (NLT), we read a very interesting statement. "Even though Jesus was God's Son, he learned obedience from the things he suffered." And so will we. The apostle Paul gave us a glimpse of what it means to know Christ. This request was not only Paul's prayer, but the cry of his heart. "That I may know Him and the power of His resurrection, and the fellowship of His sufferings, being conformed to His death, if, by any means, I may attain to the resurrection from the dead" (Philippians 3:10–11).

None of us can easily rejoice over our sufferings. I would never attempt to tell my family that they should be happy over the tragedy they endured. Rejoicing in God has nothing to do with happiness. The things we gain from walking with God are so much deeper, wider, and higher than we can wrap our minds around. They are spiritual truths that only a spiritual mind can absorb. His ways

*Have I ever used my pain to climb to a higher place in God?*

and His words are so much higher than ours, and we must not diminish their significance because of our lack of understanding. Simply put, there are things we will not understand this side of heaven, and suffering is one of them. Yet for the things we don't understand, we have Christ—the Healer of broken hearts.

What we often do not realize is that for a child of God, our great enemy is at work to get us down and keep us down. Because suffering from the loss of a loved one is systemic and affects every part of us, Satan uses it against us. He enhances our pain many times over when we are weak and hurting. He is the father of lies, and when something has been said or done that hurts us, he magnifies it over and over. You know the routine. We think about a certain scenario and then rehearse it in our minds again and again—the pain growing each time. It is similar to removing a scab from a sore before it is fully healed. We reopen that wound, and it takes longer to heal.

I am so very thankful for the support people that I had in my life—a best friend, a sweet sister, a strong brother, my sons and daughters-in-law, and many others who walked this road with me. But it was my relationship with my loving and caring Savior that brought me through the darkness and out on the other side.

During my time of recovery, I allowed myself to do what I could do and not what others thought I should do. Among other things, I gave myself permission not to attend funerals for a period of time. I literally craved time alone. Because I wasn't sleeping well, I was awake every day by 3:00 a.m. and spent the next four to five hours with God. I wrote. I cried. I prayed. I walked and talked with my Lord. My tear-stained journals are full of anguish, grief, and sorrow, but they are also full of thanksgiving and praise to a God who never left me alone. I found myself singing over and over the popular song "My Life Is in You, Lord."[1] The songwriter declares that not only is his life in the Lord, but his strength and hope are as well. It became my theme song, the story of my life, the very essence of how I continued to breathe through the most difficult days.

With each chorus, I declared that my life was now in Him, and it was. Everything I was or ever hoped to be was in Christ. He would be my future. It took me several years to actually begin to feel like a whole human being again, but it did happen in time. And it will happen for you too. We simply must learn to care for what has been wounded. We must learn the careful tending of our souls because our souls matter.

As I slowly began to put my life back in order, I defined who I was in writing—who I was today and how I would spend the rest of my life. This was my way of affirming who I was *after* my loss. I would no longer listen to the lies of the enemy. I would be who God tells me that I am according to His Word. "The rarest treasures of life are found in His truth" (Psalm 19:10 TPT).

Each line of my affirmation represents a battle that I had fought during my struggle. Each negative and painful place I had found myself in was replaced by a positive affirmation of who I was with God's firm grip on my hand. All of the accusations the enemy of my soul had taunted me with were countered with biblically supported words of strength and faith. The trajectory of my life was now headed in a new direction—with God as my constant guide and protector. I would no longer be spiraling downward; I would be looking up and forward while holding the hand of my God. These words of faith flowed easily through my pen and landed on the page:

## Holding the Hand of God

The road may be rocky, but I'll not stumble.
Fiery darts may be hurdled, but they'll
    not penetrate my life.
Storm clouds may darken the sky, but I'll
    come out on the other side.
The whole world may look hopeless,
    but it is not my home.
For I shall run and not be weary; I
    shall walk and not faint,
While holding the hand of God.

Therefore, my hope is sure.
My light is shining.
My way is bright.
My heart is steady.
My faith is strong.
My peace is unexplainable,
And my world is safe
While holding the hand of God.

My will is surrendered.
My motives are pure.
My vision is clear.
My mind is set.
My purpose is determined.
My goal is reachable,
And my agenda is His agenda
While holding the hand of God.

My strength is renewed.
My wisdom is from above.
My thoughts are just.
My words are full of grace.
My meditations are acceptable.

My song is filled with praise,
And my only desire is to please Him
While holding the hand of God.

Tending to our wounds is delicate work, and it is necessary. We are left here for a reason, and it is important that our lives are healthy and usable to the Master for whatever that reason may be. Please understand that my words of affirmation can be your words as well. God is no respecter of persons, and what He does for one, He will do for all. Truly, He found me and rescued me from my dark days of suffering, and He will find you and rescue you too. He has not promised that we will never go through painful times, but He has promised to walk with us when we do. As we head down the road to recovery with Him, He offers us His strong hand. It is ours for the taking. And with His hand in ours, we have nothing to fear.

These marvelous statements from God's Word give us hope: "He heals the wounds of every shattered heart" (Psalm 147:3 TPT). "You have turned my mourning into joyful dancing. You have taken away my clothes of mourning and clothed me with joy, that I might sing praises to you and not be silent" (Psalm 30:11–12 NLT).

Take the very hardest thing in your life the place of difficulty, outward or inward, and expect God to triumph gloriously in that very spot. Just there He can bring your soul into blossom.[2] —Lilias Trotter

CHAPTER TEN

# THE TRIUMPH

What does this tragedy have to say to us today? What does any tragedy have to say to us? It is not that "time will heal," because it won't. It's not that "you'll be better when you get your mind off it," because that rarely happens. It is not even that "you must not allow tragedy to define you," because it can't unless you allow it, and chances are that you might do that very thing. But this tragic story and any tragic story have this one thing to say to us: *There is life after tragedy.* We need look no further than Christ's cross to prove this truth. It is also true that *there is life after your tragedy.*

Tragedies happen every day. I see a tragedy in the face of every person diagnosed with cancer and in every child with metachromatic leukodystrophy (MLD) or any other life-altering disease. I see tragedy in every unwanted baby born or discarded, in every horrendous crime against another human being, in every sexual offense or depraved action that defames a life, and in every twisted thing that attempts to mar God's crowned creation so that they almost no longer look human. I also see great tragedy in every muddled mind that believes there is no God.

The psalmist David said in Psalm 14:1, "The fool has said in his heart, 'there is no God.'" Of course, there is a God. Without a God, there is no hope of a better tomorrow, and without hope of a better tomorrow, there is no hope at all. Our very existence is proof there is a God. Everything we see, including ourselves, leads to renewal and regeneration, and that in itself is proof there is a God. Every sunrise and every sunset add more proof. Every tree, every flower, every raindrop, every newborn thing, every new day, and every new beginning stacks up as evidence. The sun, the moon, and the stars all say the same thing: there is a Creator. The mountains, the rivers, and the seas all speak to us. Every bird that sings and every song that's sung is melodious confirmation. "For ever since the world was created, people have seen the earth and sky. Through everything God made, they can clearly see his invisible qualities—his eternal power and divine nature. So, they have no excuse for not knowing God" (Romans 1:20 NLT).

A poem of praise by King David found in Psalm 19 also tells of God's story being written in the skies. This marvelous display leaves us no room to doubt.

> God's splendor is a tale that is told;
> his testament is written in the stars.
> Space itself speaks his story every day
> through the marvels of the heavens.
> His truth is on tour in the starry vault of the sky,
> showing his skill in creation's craftsmanship.
> Each day gushes out its message to the next,
> night with night whispering its knowledge to all.
> Without a sound, without a word, without a voice being heard,
> Yet all the world can see its story.
> Everywhere its gospel is clearly read so all may know.
> (Psalm 19:1–4 TPT)

We have no excuse for not knowing God.

- All of creation tells us He is there.
- All of creation tells us He is here.
- All of creation tells us He knows.
- All of creation tells us He cares.

*Even if it takes a tragedy to get us to listen.*

Too often, it is only in desperate times that we look beyond ourselves and catch a glimpse of the Creator. Sometimes, when our need for God surpasses every other need in life, we finally cry out to Him.

## A Deeper Cause

God doesn't waste anything. He uses every morsel of our pain, our heartache, and our despair to turn our attention toward Him. He speaks volumes through throbbing hearts so He can point us to eternity. Yet it is our wounded souls that need so desperately to hear what He has to say to us.

God cares about our physical sickness—our brokenness and our diseases—but He longs most to heal our soul-sickness. *Our healing has a greater purpose than to simply stop our pain.* Read that statement again. In fact, doctors tell us that pain is a good thing. It lets us know that something in our body is not normal. A high temperature tells us that our child has more going on than meets the eye and prods us to look deeper for the cause.

God's dealings point us toward a deeper cause as well. His message to us will always be an eternal one, for it is the healing of our souls that ultimately matters to our Maker. We are all wounded. Every offspring of Adam and Eve is broken. We all need healing, and only the wounded Jesus can heal our deep woundedness.

Christ's call "Come to me," as found in Matthew 11:28, can be heard by all who are listening. There are times when our pain is so great that it's hard for us to hear His invitation, yet He repeatedly calls to us. Christ alone knows how to fix our neediness—how futile are our efforts to try to fix ourselves. The best plan of action is to run to God, admit our helplessness, and plead for Him to do the work in us. I've seen it in my own life—running to God in desperation and allowing Him to do the work. And I've seen it in the lives of my family. God brought my parents, my aunts and uncles, and my cousins through every hard thing. They are proof that God is indeed the Healer of open, bleeding wounds.

*Our healing has a greater purpose than to simply stop our pain.*

There is a pathway to triumph, and Christ Himself will be the One to lead us to that place. Counselors and clergy can certainly help us learn to cope with the quagmire of unanswered questions, but only God can bring us out on the other side of tragedy.

So now we get it. Tragedy happens, and we cannot change it, try as we may. But we also need to grasp that triumph happens too. I've walked that pathway—the pathway to triumph. Knowing now what my family members endured and also knowing how they lived their lives *after* their tragedy, I am certain they came out on the other side as well.

For years I watched the news commentator Charles Krauthammer on *Fox News Evening Report with Bret Baier.* He was an extraordinary man who sat at the news desk in a wheelchair. One would hardly notice it, unless you knew his story. Charles had sustained an incapacitating neck injury in a diving accident when he was a young man in college. It didn't stop him though as he went ahead to finish his degree to become a doctor. Later, he chose to enter journalism and gained great acclaim for his work. A few weeks before the well-known doctor, journalist, best-selling author, and Pulitzer Prize winner died in 2018, he wrote to his friends and colleagues that he had no regrets—because he had lived the life he intended. In spite of severe handicaps, he still did everything in life he wanted to do. His good friend Bret Baier described him like this: "Charles lived life as if the accident never happened."[1]

## Making a Comeback

How do deeply wounded people make a comeback and live as if the thing—the accident, the betrayal, the calamity, the tragedy—never happened? *They do it one step at a time, with the help of their Creator.* We must first believe that triumph can be ours. It does not happen just because we want it to or because we think we deserve it. Nor does it happen because we ask for it, pray for it, or beg for it. Triumph comes slowly and methodically as we pursue it with an intentional, unwavering determination to live again—just as if it never happened. A comeback occurs something like this:

> There is triumph when we get out of bed the morning after our tragedy, and the next, and the next, and for the rest of our lives.
> There is triumph when we face another day believing there is a good reason that we do.

There is triumph when we put one foot in front of the other with the intention of propelling ourselves forward.

There is triumph when we grieve yet have the hope of better days ahead.

There is triumph when we refuse to believe the lies of defeat and discouragement.

There is triumph when we declare that God cares about us regardless of how we feel.

There is triumph when each day is a little less dark than the one before.

There is triumph when we give our sorrows to God for the 10,000th time.

There is triumph when we choose to live again even if we're not sure we want to.

There is triumph when we believe that the Giver of Life will give *life to us.*

There is triumph when we can accept what God has allowed to happen.

Author Priscilla Shirer writes, "Whatever He's given or not given, He's done for a specific reason."[2] Because of God's good and unchangeable character, I've learned to trust that whatever He allows in my life is of value in His kingdom. He doesn't allow pain and suffering for no reason at all. It will always be used to train us, strengthen us, or shape us, and that will always bring Him glory. On this fact, we can rest.

As we slowly make our way through the grieving process and on toward triumph, we will grow to trust that His reasons are in our eternal best interest. Recovery is always a *choice*—a choice we will eventually have to make, unless we choose *not* to respond to the healing God offers us. If we choose a victim mentality, we will never move beyond our wounds to a place of victory. On the other hand, if we choose to be an overcomer, God will enable us to overcome our woundedness.

Even though we overcome our wounds, we will still have our scars. They will serve as reminders of what we've been through, just as Jesus has the scars of nail prints in His hands and feet. When we look back at our times of deep sorrow, we will be reminded just how far we have come.

Best-selling author Sheila Walsh wrote this about her scars: "If Christ has chosen to live eternally with His scars, why would I be ashamed to show mine?"[3] We shouldn't be ashamed either. And when we look at those scars many years later, we will find ourselves giving praise and glory to God for the great things He has done for us.

You may be thinking right now that giving God glory for your tragedy will never happen. It seems impossible, considering your current feelings. Yet I'm reminded of a young, single mom I watched walk through the grueling process of losing a child to MLD (metachromatic leukodystrophy), a rare and progressive disease that currently has no cure. Carrie loves God with all her heart. When I first met her, she had already adopted one child through her state's Department of Child and Family Services, a beautiful, biracial child. But she wanted more children. She

*If we choose a victim mentality, we will never move beyond our wounds to a place of victory.*

continued to pray for God to open that door for another child, but several years passed before her prayer was answered. And then it happened. Carrie was allowed to adopt two newborns: a baby boy and a baby girl just one month apart. Her nest was full, and although she continued to work full time, she loved and adored her brood of three precious children unwanted by their biological parents.

As her little boy reached the age of two, it became increasingly apparent that something was wrong. After much testing, he was given the diagnosis of MLD along with the horrifying statistics that MLD sufferers have very short life spans—especially when diagnosed early in life. That would be the case with Carrie's son. Because of her church family, her work family, and community and social media friends, I can easily say there were thousands of people praying for her and her son. Yet every day that went by, he lost the ability to do another activity—walk, talk, stand, crawl, eat, or play—until he was a near vegetable.

I continued to follow her journey on Facebook, even though it grew more difficult with each post. Many times, I stopped what I was doing and prayed for them, asking God to heal this beautiful, little boy. Two months after his third birthday, he slipped into eternity. The day Carrie posted a picture of his tiny casket, I thought I couldn't bear any more. Yet her support group of friends and family had held her up in prayer, because her heart would have failed her otherwise.

It had been grueling to watch the days following his passing. Her visits to the cemetery on special days, and many nonspecial days, were also painful. His toy dump trucks and garbage trucks that he had loved so much are part his grave decor. By anyone's measuring stick, this was a tragedy. But it doesn't stop there. Carrie belonged to a support group for MLD children, and every few months, another precious child is taken from this life. The grief never seems to end for my sweet friend.[4]

Carrie's questions are many, and so are mine. Why would God give and then take away? Why wouldn't it have been better if this child had never come into her life or even into the world? What could possibly have been the purpose for such pain? In God's good time, I know Carrie will find the comfort and perhaps even the answers that she needs because God is faithful. In the meanwhile, she is walking really close to her Savior. It's not important that she understands it now or ever.

I don't understand it either, but I know that in this little boy's three short years on earth, God chose to give him the best home and the best momma any little boy could hope to have. He was loved and cherished every moment of his short existence. He was adored by grandparents, aunts and uncles, cousins, and two loving sisters who cared for him, played with him, read to him, sang to him, and made his every wish come true. God knew all along how short his life would be, and He gave him the most loving and caring family on the face of the earth!

Like Carrie, most of us may never understand this side of heaven why our tragedy happened or who might be changed for eternity because of our tragedy. It isn't always intended that we know the *why* or the *who*. The Bible tells us plainly, "Now we see things imperfectly, like puzzling reflections in a mirror, but then we will see everything with perfect clarity. All that I know now is partial and incomplete, but then I will know everything completely, just as God now knows me completely" (1 Corinthians 13:12 NLT).

It is by our faith that we move forward at all—trusting God *as* we go. Tiny steps are acceptable—in fact, most desirable. It is a slow process. God is in no hurry whatsoever, and we shouldn't be either. We have to give God time to do His intricate work in our hearts, and we have to give ourselves time to respond to His gentle hand.

Amy Carmichael, missionary to India, wrote, "Are we made perfect in a day? The cloud that makes the pastures green is a good cloud. The rainbow of the love of God is set in every cloud that ever darkens our sky. Clouds and rainbows work together for the perfecting of our souls."[5]

It is helpful to understand that our cooperation and participation in our recovery are important to God. Oswald Chambers said it like this: "God does not give us overcoming life—He gives us life as we overcome."[6]

And we must remember to leave yesterday where it belongs: behind us. "I must go forward where I have never been instead of backwards where I have,"[7] said Winnie the Pooh. That is wise advice for any of us. It will help us propel ourselves into the future, and that is where we must go.

## Trusted with a Tragedy

I expect that if we had the supernatural ability and the privilege of looking back on every tragedy that God has allowed on earth, we may see victories in the lives of those who suffered greatly. It has always been true that God takes what Satan meant for evil and turns it around to be something good. God is the Master of everything. While He does not cause tragedies, He masterfully uses the results of tragedies for eternal value.

Remember that we may never know the why or the who God is trying to reach through our tragedy, but I know some who were reached with the tragedy of my grandparents. At the time of the tragedy in 1946, only one daughter and her husband were serving the Lord. Yet today, we can perhaps see the end results of my grandparents' godly lives, as well as their untimely death. All of their children, including spouses, and all of their eight grandchildren became followers of Christ, as well as many great- and great-great-grandchildren.

My grandmother had made the statement that she would rather die than lock her son away in a mental institution, and that is exactly what happened. Her son had a mental illness for which there were no cures or treatments. Leo Bode knew the God of his parents, because it was to God he cried out only days before he lost control of himself. It was a nearly impossible situation. We do not know what God might have done to stop any of it. We just know that He didn't.

So what did God do? Anything? Oh yes, He did something. He trusted this family with a tragedy—a tragedy that shook hundreds and maybe thousands of lives. I believe that all who heard it paused to consider their own eternal destiny. I am confident that the moment my grandparents and uncle drew their last breaths, they were with God in heaven. Eternal things are always top priority with God. They should be with us as well. If our trials, tribulations, or tragedies can be used by the Heavenly Father to speak to those who do not know Him, then so be it. It shook my precious family members to the core, such that none of them dared to miss heaven.

That, my friend, is what triumph looks like.

The missionary to India Amy Carmichael, who spoke of the clouds and rainbows working together, was herself trusted with a tragedy. After taking a crippling fall, she never walked again. She spent the last seventeen years of her life in bed. Her words speak deeply about her unshakable trust in God. "Our God trusts us to trust Him. Let us not disappoint God. Let us rise to this great trust."[8]

Because I believe God uses us for His eternal purposes, the prayer for my own life should go something like this: "Father, help me trust what You have for me in the here and now yet also in the light of eternity, for what I do today impacts eternity in my life and in the lives of others."

> The catastrophe that awaits everyone from a single false move, wrong turn, fatal encounter—every life has such a moment. What distinguishes us is whether—and how—we ever come back.[9] —Charles Krauthammer

CHAPTER ELEVEN

# THE EXCHANGE

There is an exchange involved in most everything we do in life. Employers pay employees for the work they perform. We pay money for products and services we want and need. We devote ourselves to a particular field of study and earn a degree. We place our money in various investments and get returns (hopefully). Give and get. Give and take. Exchange happens every day in a thousand ways.

I can't help but think about the exchange that was made between me and my first cousins and what each gave and received throughout the process. I'm not sure we ever thought we'd actually be here—talking openly about our grandparents' tragedy. Yet God has brought it about, and I see several things that have been exchanged along the way.

For my cousins, I believe the greatest benefit for them has been in sharing the pain that their tragedy caused them for so many years. Perhaps a miracle happened back in chapter 2: "The Gathering," when those floodgates opened and healing began to flow as they each told their stories. I'm certain there were times throughout their lives when they thought the pain would never go away. Yet they learned to manage it because life would certainly move on. Life always moves on, whether we choose to go with it or not. They went on, as did their parents. I am so grateful for their openness and honesty. It has made the story come alive—our seeing it through their eyes. I believe God will use their courage to help others walking a similar road.

For me, my two siblings, and Elaine, we have in a sense been given the gift of grandparents. I had once thought our grandparents were grandparents to only those cousins who knew them. Yet I now believe that I will know my grandparents when I get to heaven. I also enjoy the things I now know about them—what they were like, how they lived and loved their grandchildren, and how "the Lord was their life." I especially enjoyed learning about my family's gift of music. It helps me better understand me.

The exchange has been worth whatever it cost any of us: time, tears, or tension. We did it. Together we unpacked our story and have shared it with the world as well as with other families who have suffered a tragedy.

## A Greater Exchange

There is another exchange that took place long before any of us were born. It began with God and His great love—an exchange that has much to say to all of us.

Every time we open ourselves up to love, we are opening ourselves up to pain. It is much like the old song "Love and Marriage"[1] that tells us those two things are linked together just like a horse and carriage are linked together. Love and pain also go together, even if we don't want to believe it is true.

The opportunity for pain to enter our lives comes through the door with whomever or whatever we choose to love. When we allow a person or a thing, such as a pet, to occupy space in our hearts, we are setting ourselves up for a painful loss when that person or thing is removed. Their departure will leave a gaping hole for a period of time that nothing else can fill—and for the most part,

*Love and pain also go together, even if we don't want to believe it is true.*

we choose not to fill. It is also true that the more we love, the more pain we will endure. So why do we do this to ourselves? Why do we love another?

We take the risk of loving because, like Alfred, Lord Tennyson so eloquently stated in his famous poem, "'Tis better to have loved and lost than never to have loved at all."[2] In other words, the pain of loss does not outweigh the pleasure of love. It's worth it! It's worth every ounce of pain to have given love and to have been loved in return. Many a lover with a broken heart will testify to that very thing. That's why we take the plunge into the great unknown at a marriage altar or in a hospital delivery room. We make plans to marry our Princess or Prince Charming with whom we pledge to live happily ever after. Then we choose to bring children into our home and have visions of grandeur as we watch our clan swell into one big, happy family. We let our hearts run wild with love—because we believe it will be worth it.

The process of deciding to love another at a cost to ourselves is a transaction or an exchange. We give our love now at the cost of experiencing pain sometime in the future. You can do the math: love now equals pain later. That is an exchange of two things. We should know the cost up front, but we don't. We take the plunge anyway.

It's interesting to consider that in the beginning before God ever made man, He fully knew the cost up front to love us. Nevertheless, He chose to create us, and it would be a great exchange of both love and pain. The Bible tells us the Ephesians 1:3–11 (NLT) exactly what God's plan was. (I have italicized the words that support my theory.)

> All praise to God, the Father of our Lord Jesus Christ, who has blessed us with every spiritual blessing in the heavenly realms because we are united with Christ. *Even before he made the world, God loved us and chose us* in Christ to be holy and without fault in his eyes. *God decided in advance to adopt us into his own family* by bringing us to himself through Jesus Christ. *This is what he wanted to do, and it gave him great pleasure.* So we praise God for the glorious grace he has poured out on us who belong to his dear Son. He is so rich in kindness and grace that *he purchased our freedom with the blood of his Son* and forgave our sins. He has showered his kindness on us, along with all wisdom and understanding. God has now revealed to us his mysterious will regarding Christ—*which is to fulfill his own good plan.* And this is the plan: At the right time he will bring everything together under the authority of Christ—everything in heaven and on earth. Furthermore,

because we are united with Christ, we have received an inheritance from God, for *he chose us in advance, and he makes everything work out according to his plan.*

We should never make the mistake of thinking we were an accident. Never. God knew exactly what He was doing all along—before the foundation of the world. He chose to love us because it gave Him pleasure, even at the cost of His Son's own blood. Let that sink in. Love and pain were clearly linked in God's great plan, so why did He agree to such an exchange? Because it is always, always, always *better* to love and lose than never to love at all!

The alternative of *not* loving is never the better choice—even if our pain is extreme. Think about what it will be like with millions upon millions of God's children sharing heaven with our Heavenly Father, our Beloved Savior, and the precious Holy Spirit. As God considered His plan to make human beings, knowing that we would mess up, He still took the risk of loving us because the pain does not outweigh the pleasure of love.

No doubt there would be pain in the future—a dreadfully dark day when Jesus would offer His life for our sins and pay the cost to set us free from our own doing. Yet Christ did it willingly because He too wanted someone to share heaven with. He loved us that much. The pain would surely be worth it all. If we could only grasp how much God loves us, how much He longs for our fellowship, our time, our attention, and our love in return! If only we could see God as He really is—taking a huge risk to love us because of His great loneliness and a love that could not be satisfied any other way.

Cory Ashbury, songwriter and recording artist of the 2018 award-winning song "Reckless Love," captures God's love so perfectly. He writes,

> The same God who created heaven and earth—gives Himself away in desperate hopes that we'll return His love … God's longing to be loved isn't a suspension of His power; it's evidence of the incomprehensible fury of His love.[3]

## The Greatest Exchange of All Time

But there is yet another exchange for us to consider. We might describe it as the greatest exchange of all time. In several verses found in Romans 5, we have a very clear picture of what God has done for us—if we will accept the exchange. Read these passages while asking God for eyes to see, as if you've never read them before. I have chosen The Passion Translation because of its amazing clarity.

> Our faith in Jesus transfers God's righteousness to us and he now declares us flawless in his eyes. This means we can now enjoy true and lasting peace with God, all because of what our Lord Jesus, the Anointed One, has done for us. Our faith guarantees us permanent access into this marvelous kindness that has given us a perfect relationship with God. What incredible joy bursts forth within us as we keep on celebrating our hope of experiencing God's glory! (Romans 5:1–2 TPT)

> But Christ proved God's passionate love for us by dying in our place while we were still lost and ungodly! And there is still much more to say of his unfailing love for us! For through the blood of Jesus we have heard the powerful declaration, "You are now righteous in my sight." And because of the sacrifice of Jesus, you will never experience the wrath of God. So if while we were still enemies, God fully reconciled us to himself through the death of his Son, then something greater than friendship is ours. Now that we are at peace with God, and because we share in his resurrection life, how much more we will be rescued from sin's dominion! And even more than that, we overflow with triumphant joy in our new relationship of living in harmony with God—all because of Jesus Christ! (Romans 5:8–11 TPT)

It is interesting that the verb *reconciled* used in this passage actually means "exchanged" in the Greek language. This powerful scripture allows us to see clearly what God offers to us in this exchange—those things of value: righteousness, acquittal for our sins, true and lasting peace with God, marvelous kindness, incredible joy, reconciliation, and resurrection life.

Did you happen to notice at the very beginning of this passage what our side of the bargain might be? What thing of value does God wants from us in order to complete this exchange? You got it. God is looking for *faith!* His requirement has never changed, from the Old Testament until this very day—God is still looking for *faith!* Everything we get from God is given because we believe He provides it and wants to give it to us. Everything! No ladders to climb, no good grades to make, no perfect attendance trophies. None! Nada! Nothing!

Just *faith!*

Let's look at a scripture that confirms this concept. It describes the covenant God made with Abraham, who is known as the Father of *faith.*

> God promised Abraham and his descendants that they would have an heir who would reign over the world. This royal promise was not fulfilled because Abraham kept all the law, but through the righteousness that was transferred by faith. (Romans 4:13 TPT)

> The promise depends on faith so that it can be experienced as a grace-gift, and now it extends to all of the descendants of Abraham. (Romans 4:16 TPT)

I believe that faith is the currency of heaven—the only thing that we can trade to God in exchange for anything we might want or need from Him. He simply asks us to believe that He will give it, and He does. It is one of the mysteries of the gospel. The writer of Hebrews defines this great truth for us.

> And without faith living within us it would be impossible to please God. For we come to God in faith knowing that he is real and that he rewards the faith of those who give all their passion and strength into seeking him. (Hebrews 11:6 TPT)

Our God is, in fact, a great risk-taker. Not only did He risk the pain of sending His Son to die a horrific death to rescue us, but He also decided to give us a choice in the matter. If we want to accept God's amazing gift of love and acquittal, then there is something we must do. It is somewhat like buying a car. You pick it out, test drive it, and decide you want it, but some exchange must take place for you to own it and drive it home. It is the same with

*Have you ever seen yourself as the prize? Well, you are. So believe it!*

our salvation. *Things of value must be exchanged.* So what will it be? Our faith exchanged for His great grace-gift of resurrection life along with a host of other benefits. What a deal!

If by any chance it seems to you that this exchange is highly lopsided, you are correct! Things are *always* lopsided in our favor with our generous God. In fact, I have learned throughout my Christian experience that there is no way we can ever outgive His generosity. He doesn't wait until we earn it, get it right, or learn our lesson. He simply gives abundantly.

The apostle John defined God's abundant love so accurately when he wrote, "Behold, what manner of love the Father has bestowed on us, that we should be called the children of God" (1 John 3:1).

## What to Do with Our Pain

"There is no normal life that is free of pain,"[4] said Mr. Rogers. Even as born-again believers having received God's great gift of salvation, we are not exempt from the pain of life on earth. We live, we love, and we take risks, yet we also lose, we grow old, and sometimes we face tragedy. The storybook picture of Dick and Jane doesn't always turn out picture-perfect. When life happens, we have pain. The better question is perhaps not what we are going to do with our pain but what we *can* do with our pain.

God turned the pain Christ endured on the cross into something positive—us! As born-again believers, we are the prize Christ won on Calvary. Have you ever seen yourself as the prize? Well, you are. So believe it! You and I are the prize. Since Christ's love bought us on a pain-filled cross, we could say it was a tragedy turned positive. Christ's pain traded for our love. Unthinkable! Are we lavishly bestowing our love back on the Savior? Are we making Christ's pain worth it? If not, we should be. We should be pouring out our love on Him every hour of every day. We will be doing that very thing throughout all eternity!

What then can you and I do with the pain from our tragedy? Don't you just love that old multiple-option theory that always begins with "Number one: You can do nothing"? I'm sorry, but doing nothing as a child of God will never work. Our God is *not* a "do nothing" kind of God. He is a "do something God"! He is a God of action, a God of life, a God of the living, a miracle-working God, a victorious God, and an overcoming God. He parts seas, feeds thousands with small lunches, walks on water, raises dead bodies, heals diseases, causes blind eyes to see, and saves the souls of men because He loves us extravagantly. So let's take the "do nothing" option off the table.

I see two viable things we can do with our pain: we can keep it, or we can give it away. If we choose to keep it, we'll likely have to carry it with us until we reach the end of life's road. It mirrors the story of the man walking along the road while carrying a heavy backpack. When an old trucker drove up beside the man, he stopped and offered the man a ride. The man graciously accepted and jumped on the back of the truck. However, he continued to carry the backpack on his shoulder, allowing the weight of it to rest on himself. When another rider on the truck asked why he was still carrying the backpack, he said that the truck driver had been so kind in offering him a ride that he couldn't let him carry the backpack too.

The problem with carrying our backpack full of pain and sorrow to heaven with us is that we will eventually have to leave it at heaven's gate— for pain and sorrow cannot enter there. And once inside, we will see the foolishness of having carried it for so long, just as the man who continued to bear that weight on his shoulder. God never intended for us to carry such burdens, for Christ is indeed our burden bearer.

On the other hand, God offers us a much better option. We can give our pain and sorrow to Him because He is also a transforming God. He takes our nothingness, our worthlessness, our sins, our sorrows, and our pain and does something with them. That is what He did with Christ's pain. He transformed it into something. That something was eternal life for us.

In 2004, the January following the death of my husband, I had just survived my first Christmas without him. I gained a greater compassion for all who struggle to endure the holidays, be it months or years since their loss. My own pain was magnified many times over as I had lost twenty people—family, friends, or other cancer patients—during that year. I had come to know by experience that pain is part of life, and on this day, God dealt with my heart about my pain. In His love and kindness, He offered me something I could do with my pain. Here is how I described the exchange that was offered to me.

### Pain Transformed (An Excerpt from My Journal)

A few months ago, I was given a book called *What the Cross Means to Me.*[5] It is a collection of writings by various well-known Christian authors on the meaning of the cross to their lives. It had blessed me tremendously, yet I was most moved by the photographs in the book. They are pictures of a cross—the same cross—from different angles and with different backdrops.

In the front of the book is an explanation by the photographer, Rob Holt, which tells how the photographs came to be. Rob and his wife, Verna, had an up-and-coming business when Verna learned that she had colon cancer. Two *days* later, at the age of twenty-four, Verna was dead. Rob's life went into shock. He lost everything they had worked for. He was forced to make major changes in his job. In his quest to deal with his pain, Rob began taking long walks along a lonely hillside near his home to watch the sun go down in the evenings. It was there that Rob felt closest to God. Next he picked back up his true love of life—photography—and began capturing the magnificent beauty of those sunsets.

Sometime later, a friend invited Rob on a hike that led him to a twelve-foot cross mounted atop a quiet and peaceful slope. As Rob began to find the peace he longed for, he built a collection of photographs of that cross with various skyscapes. The collection is profound. Today, as I enjoy this precious little book, I realized that had God not taken Verna Holt to heaven when He did, Rob would never have made this collection of photographs that have blessed my life tremendously and the lives of countless others.

As I consider my pain over the past year, I now realize there is something I can do with my pain. *When our pain is given to God, it can be transformed into something that will bless others. Is that not the central message of Christ's cross—pain transformed?*

Oh yes, it is! Christ's suffering was pain transformed into mercy, grace, forgiveness, redemption, and eternal life—all for me and for you. In the light of that revelation, I would have to say that the cross means *everything* to me.

## God's Offer to His Children

Our Loving God makes a great offer to all of His children who are experiencing pain. That offer is found in Matthew 11:28 (NLT). "Come to me, all of you who are weary and carry heavy burdens, and I will give you rest." We can continue to carry our pain and He will help us do that, or we can give our pain to Him. Once we put it into His hands, He has the ability to transform it into something that will bless others. It could be one of the greatest exchanges we will ever make—something we don't want to keep (pain and sorrow) in exchange for something of great worth (blessing others).

If it is true that God uses our pain to bless others, can we conclude that God took Verna Holt so I could be blessed? Not necessarily, because we do not know why God took Verna to heaven. But since He did take her from this life, we know what God did with Rob's pain. He transformed it to something that brought glory to Himself.

The truth is that none of us know what God might do with our transformed pain. Just as Rob's photographs are pictures of a cross—the same cross—from different angles and with different backdrops, so are our tragedies. We all bear the same cross of pain and suffering, yet the angles and backdrops are totally different. They are akin to snowflakes: no two tragedies are alike because tragedies come in all shapes and sizes. They affect us in drastically different ways. Your story may impact people my story could never reach.

While we simply do not know how God could use our pain, here are a few ideas. He could use it to help people with similar pain find comfort and relief. He could use it to reach someone considering suicide because their pain is no longer bearable. He could use it to give hope to thousands who could benefit from your story of a rescuing God. He could use it to bring many souls into the kingdom to share heaven with us. The glorious possibilities are endless because our glorious God is always drawing people to Himself, and the amazing thing for us is that He is always using His children to do so.

## The Final Exchange

Some day in our future, there will be yet another exchange—when our journey on earth comes to an end. There is no fear at life's end because it will be an exchange unlike any we have ever made before. Author Calvin Miller describes it in a most fascinating way in his book *Into the Depths of God*. I recommend reading it slowly.

> In Scripture, it (death) seems to be presented as a part of life, and certainly in the New Testament it is presented as a kind of achievement. It is the victorious end of the glorious pilgrimage. It is a changing of residence, the trading of clay for gold, the bartering of protoplasm for spirit, the exchange of temporality for immorality.[6]

I anticipate that day, for on that day, all tears, pain, sorrow, and parting from loved ones will be over. Even the memories of our difficult days on earth shall disappear. We shall see those who've gone ahead of us lining the corridors of heaven, waiting for us to arrive. I believe we shall know them just as we did on earth, and for those of us who have loved ones there that we've never met, it will be as if we have known them all along. It shall be one great reunion as we stroll through heaven while exploring all of God's dazzling creation that He has prepared for us.

Yet as glorious as it shall be, none of it will compare to the marvelous privilege we will have to fall at the feet of our Savior, lavish our love on Him, and thank Him for rescuing us. I expect that the most magnificent of all exchanges—*trading our life on earth for a new life in heaven*—will give us pause. We will wonder why we ever dreaded death. I will never forget Rev. Don Starkweather's astounding words at my mom's funeral when I was twenty-one years old. With unwavering confidence, he announced, "Death is the door to God."

For now, it isn't necessary that we identify the divine reason for our tragedy on earth, but it is necessary that we trust that God's purpose will be accomplished through whatever He has allowed. I believe tragedies are allowed only when they have a God-size purpose—unless they can ultimately bring good out of evil, turn people toward God, help us find His grace and His love, and bring glory to His name.

Is it possible that we could ever grow to the place here on earth where we see the good in our tragedy? Perhaps not through these mortal eyes we have today, but I believe that every tragedy will someday be seen through heavenly eyes.

Transition in this life is ongoing, and it is almost always painful. Yet to get to where God wants us to be will require transition, transition will require change, and change will require time. Someday we will be transitioned into who we are going to be and not who we are right now.

> Who knows why God allows heartbreak, but the answer must be important enough because God allowed His heart to break too.[7] —Ann Voskamp

# CHAPTER TWELVE

# THE LEGACY

The days had been long—seconds stretching into minutes, minutes into hours, and hours into days since the decline started. Still, she lingered. The only remaining child of Oscar and Ethel Bode, LaVerne (Nonnie) Parker, had lived for ninety-six years, and she was certainly taking her time leaving here. Carolyn had hoped the transition would be easy for her mom, yet there wasn't anything easy about this. Many years ago, my aunt had made a determined effort to live—and not die—after the tragic events of June 25, 1946. And live she did! In fact, she had outlived them all: her parents, her three brothers, and one sister. Perhaps it was that same determination that held her earthbound through these grueling and lingering days.

But in another place—on a faraway shore—I vision the minutes, hours, and days were drawn out as well. Just as her earthly family was watching her departure, her heavenly family was watching for her arrival. When would she come? How much longer until this one remaining sister makes it home? Then at last, on April 13, 2015, she took her final breath, and she too crossed over into that fair heaven. On this glorious day, Aunt Nonnie would see them all: Oscar, Ethel, Floy, Leo, Hallis, and Cecil. This family of seven would be together again.

I try to imagine the joy of the reunion that was taking place on the other side. It's only with eyes of faith that I can see any of it. Oscar's favorite—his baby girl—had finally come home. With her coming, she ended the painful separation that occurred here on earth. The Oscar Bode family circle was complete again on that beautiful day that dawned in heaven. I expect there was great rejoicing like we've have never seen before—just pure joy. So much to say to each other. So much to remember. So much to explain. Would there be enough time to say it all? But then, this is their eternal home where there will be no end and no parting—ever again. Will there be singing? Certainly, the angels were singing at her arrival. But what about this singing family? Will they sing together again? My heart says yes!

There were many more members of the Bode, McDonald, and Parker families who made up the great clouds of witnesses who greeted her on this homecoming day: her husband, my mom, nieces and nephews, and many more. Still, back on earth, our hearts were breaking at the departure of this sweetest person in the whole world. She had blessed the lives of a multitude of people; her kindness was unsurpassed, and her faith was unshakeable. She too had become a pillar of stability for the family. We still needed her and were not ready to let her go.

It was the evening of the day of her funeral that Elaine called me and asked if I would write our family's story. Since that day, we have indeed captured the story from our cousins' recollections. However, there is still one thing to do: honor those who were trusted with a tragedy yet lived as if the accident never happened.

## The Greatest Generation

The generation to which my parents, aunts, and uncles belonged has been referred to as "the greatest generation." They are defined as being born from 1900 through the 1920s—those who lived through the Great Depression and fought in World War II. Yet I wonder if there was something in our parents' lives that is nearly extinct today. What has happened to integrity, hard work, character, courage, honesty, respect for others, honoring parents, faith in God, and protecting a good name? Those are things our parents and grandparents worked hard to instill in their children. Are not those very things part of our legacy? Billy Graham said, "The legacy we leave is not just in our possessions, but in the quality of our lives."[1]

One of the subtle ways I could convince my two young sons to behave appropriately was to bring out the "old family name trick," as they called it. My son, Brian, said he would rather have gotten a spanking than for Mom to pull that rabbit out of the hat. I would carefully remind them that they were a "Bode" and a "Kellogg" and that people with those names were responsible for behaving themselves accordingly. That clever trick never failed to work. Today, my boys carry those names with high regard. I just suspect that they too will be survivors in this life no matter what comes their way. I also suspect that they use Mom's old family name trick on their own children.

What are we leaving to our children: money, houses, land, and possessions? Or are we leaving a legacy of something far more valuable: character, courage, resilience, faith, and a good name? I believe some in our generation have been distracted away from teaching our children the more important things in life. We might even call them "lesser things." You know, things of lesser value in the bigger scheme of things. I fear our nation has made a great exchange in which we traded solid, rock-hard values for fleeting things that have left us in a world of want.

Our culture reeks with lesser things selling themselves as desirable. We see these things displayed on television, movies, and social media day in and day out, while God's Word tells us differently. Here are some examples of what is most valuable in God's eyes:

- Wisdom is greater than wealth.
- Peace is greater than power.
- Contentment is greater than fame.
- Joy is greater than success.
- Integrity is greater than position.
- Love is greater than popularity.
- Eternal life is greater than pleasure.

It makes me wonder what has caused this undesirable condition in our nation. Where did the values go that were worth dying for just a few generations ago? I wonder how many of the veterans from yesteryear would give their lives for the declining, selfish culture we see today? And how did we get here? What did we do with our morals? Did we spoil the next generation and fail to teach them the greater things?

Perhaps here are some of the reasons why we did it: Because we worked our way through college, we made sure our children didn't have to. Since we had to wait to buy a car until we had the money, we gave our children a car the day they turned sixteen. Because we struggled to build a 401(k), have a savings account, and money in our pocket, we handed our children whatever they wanted.

Could it be that we have done the next generation a huge disservice? I fear that many of them live with the misunderstanding that things are easy to come by and that someone will do it for them. This lack of values has fostered an attitude of ingratitude, which leads down that dangerous road to entitlement. I suspect that we are close to having "another generation … who knew neither the LORD nor what he had done for Israel" (Judges 2:10).

Zane said that she clearly remembers an adage by the founder of Bob Jones University, where she attended college many years ago. Dr. Bob Jones Sr. repeatedly told his students, "Do not sacrifice the permanent on the altar of the immediate." So much instant gratification is sought after today: we want what we want when we want it. We do not want to wait for anything. We don't want to earn a promotion. We want it given to us. We don't want to make coffee. We want Starbucks to make it. We don't want to wear hand-me-downs because we don't even know what that word means. We have lost sight of things that have lasting, eternal value for things that make us happy—*now!*

> *To pull ourselves up by our bootstraps doesn't mean we will pull ourselves up and fix ourselves, because we can't. But we pull ourselves up and run to the One who can.*

I am not a big fan of social media, and I fear it will be years before we identify the tragic effects it has had on society, especially on our children. It has become popular to put out there for the whole world to see our best "selfie," our best foot forward, our biggest and best of whatever it is we have, including what we ordered for dinner. We also put out there our troubles and misfortunes instead of dealing with them, getting over them, and moving forward. My dad would say, "Pull yourself up by your bootstraps." I believe my dad's generation would think that we have lost our way—and perhaps our sanity.

My parents, aunts, and uncles faced a tragic blow to their lives—perhaps harder than anything the vast majority of us will ever face. Yet they did pull themselves up by their bootstraps and they did get over it—at least in the eyes of their children. I can truthfully say that my life was not affected by their tragedy. Until late in my teenage years, I wasn't even aware that it had happened. My parents were loving, caring, and healthy human beings. Were they perfect? Not by any means, but they managed to hold life together for the sake of their three children. My cousins say the very same thing: building a life, making a living, birthday parties, and school events happened right on track. Life went on because that is what strong people do—and our people were strong.

"Tough times don't last for long; tough saints go on forever,"[2] wrote Calvin Miller. We always have a way through and a way out of every hard thing, if we know where to go for help. To pull ourselves up by our bootstraps doesn't mean we will pull ourselves up and fix ourselves, because we can't. But we pull ourselves up and run to the One who can. The book of Proverbs tells us, "The name of the Lord is a strong tower, the righteous run to it and are safe" (Proverbs 18:10).

## What Defines Us?

We must not be defined by the bad things we have done, the bad things that happen to us, or even the tragedies in our lives. Not one of God's faithful servants would choose that, and we shouldn't choose it either. Let's consider some examples.

Abraham would not want to be remembered for asking his wife to lie about who he was, just because he was afraid. Or Moses for losing his temper and striking the rock instead of speaking to it. Or Peter for his three denials of the Lord Jesus. I'm confident the apostle Paul would not choose to be remembered for trying to destroy the church or standing in approval at the death of Christians. These saints were great men of God by anyone's standards.

But one truth that is easy for us to overlook is that mistakes or tragedies don't get the final say in our lives. We do—through the legacy that we leave behind. I am confident that Oscar and Ethel Bode do not want to be remembered for their tragic ending. They want to be remembered for being faithful servants of God, the loving, caring, singing family that they were, and by the strong children that they raised. As those four children grew up and had families of their own, their desire was to pass on to their children the same admirable qualities that had been left to them. And Oscar and Ethel's true legacy lives on today.

## Leaving a Mark

If you are like me, you may be wondering if you're making a difference in even one human life, much less in the world. Are we leaving a mark anywhere? We want to, but our results are seemingly unimpressive. The only way we can leave a mark in the world that makes a difference is to let Christ make His mark through us. The attention goes to Him. The honor and the glory go to Him. And we are satisfied with simply having been used by the Master.

If we seek to leave a mark for ourselves, we will actually miss the mark—the goal of living a Christian life. So how do we leave a mark for God? The question has been asked before, yet most of us don't like the answer. Leaving a mark for God requires denial of self, even as Jesus denied Himself. Denying self is the way of the cross. Jesus told His disciples in Luke 9:23, "If anyone desires to come after Me, let him deny himself, and take up his cross daily, and follow Me."

In modern-day language, being a Jesus follower looks like this: give up the spotlight; don't seek rewards for yourself; don't let others know what your left hand or your right hand is doing; help those who can't help themselves; forgive first, love first, and eat last; take the smaller piece, the back seat, the worst seat, or no seat at all; and always take the shorter stick. Those are the things we do to *position* ourselves to be used of God to leave His mark on the world.

The Bible is full of examples of people who *positioned* themselves in order to find what mattered most.

- Zacchaeus risked being embarrassed by climbing a tree so he could *see* Jesus. He not only got to see Jesus, but Jesus went home with him and brought salvation to his entire house (Luke 19:1–10).
- The woman with an issue of blood stooped low and crawled on her knees so she could *touch* the hem of Jesus's garment.

This courageous act of faith led to her body being made whole (Matthew 9:20–22).

- Although Nicodemus *came* to Jesus by night, still he came, in spite of being criticized and perhaps ostracized by the Jews. His coming led to a one-on-one encounter with Christ about how to be born again (John 3:1–18).
- Blind Bartimaeus *called* out to Jesus at the risk of ridicule from others. When the crowd warned him to be quiet, he shouted louder. Jesus heard him and asked for Bartimaeus to be brought to him. The blind beggar, who had already thrown away his dignity, now "threw aside his garment" as he went to Jesus. His sight was restored (Mark 10:46–52).

All of these people desperately wanted to come into contact with the Son of God, and they did so by putting themselves in a place that required courage, determination, and faith. When they acted on their faith to *see, touch, come,* and *call* on Jesus, they opened themselves up to be used in Jesus's earthly story. Through each one of them, Jesus was able to leave

> *Position is everything—being in the right place at the right time with the right motive.*

His mark on this world, and their brave stories—and yes, their legacies—have been read by millions of people for over two thousand years.

*Position is everything—being in the right place at the right time with the right motive.* When these four people positioned themselves correctly, Jesus didn't fail to take notice. Not once! In each story, their efforts yielded a huge return. But what does correct positioning look like? The apostle Peter gives us some good advice.

> And all of you, dress yourselves in humility as you relate to one another, for "God opposes the proud but gives grace to the humble." So humble yourselves under the mighty power of God, and at the right time he will lift you up in honor. Give all your worries and cares to God, for he cares about you. (1 Peter 5:5–7 NLT)

It takes humility for a short, grown man to climb a tree so he can get a better view, a woman to stoop to the dirty ground to sneak a touch of Jesus's robe, a distinguished, high-ranking member of the Jewish temple to risk being caught, or blind Bartimaeus to make a spectacle of himself, as if he wasn't already a nuisance to society. Humility was that one common thread that ran through each of the four Bible stories. It must be present in our story as well.

All four of these desperate characters submitted themselves and their future into the hands of God—risking all they had. They saw in this moment the chance to connect with the One who might give them a thread of hope. It was their opportunity, and they weren't going to miss it—even if it cost them everything. In each case, their effort was worth the cost. It will be for us too, if we are willing to reposition ourselves.

Humility by itself is not enough. We must also have the correct motive. Motive is *why* we want what we want, and that matters to God. We may have the desire for right and noble things, such as getting healed or gaining Jesus's attention. Yet if we want it for the wrong reason, it's not likely that God will grant it. He looks on hearts and determines if we are seeking glory for ourselves or glory for Him. When our motives meet His approval, we will get to be a part of God's great story. "We were made to be prisms refracting the light of God's glory into all of life,"[3] according to John Piper.

We may invest our time making money, gaining possessions and power, or becoming famous—even if it is only with Facebook followers—but none of those things compare to the eternal value of letting God use us to tell His love story to the world. And since our time on earth is short, we must make each day count. The psalmist prayed, "Teach us to realize the brevity of life" (Psalm 90:12 NLT). We need to pray the same for ourselves.

Where does a great legacy start? It starts with you, me, or any person who gives God permission to use their lives in His story. In every generation, He writes redemption's story over and over in a thousand different ways through people desiring to leave a mark for Christ. Yet leaving our mark for Christ cannot and will not happen unless we *position* ourselves to make it happen.

And in the end, a mark for Christ is the only mark that counts.

> I do not know what each day holds, or what time I have
> left to serve. This I do know, dear Lord, I want to leave my
> mark for You. Help me make every day count. Remind me
> to lay aside my own wants, to be willingly inconvenienced
> and used for You.[4] —Anita Corrine Donihue

CHAPTER THIRTEEN

# THE END

During the 1973 National League pennant race, the American baseball legend Yogi Berra made a profound and well-known statement. "It ain't over til it's over." As reported in *BBC Magazine*, "His team was a long way behind when he said it and they did eventually rally to win the division title."[1]

Other desperate, nearly defeated human beings have used that line ever since. In spite of its grammatical errors, it is actually a statement of faith and is spoken in an effort to encourage ourselves that there is still hope. I just bet you have used it too. I know I have.

It's likely that we have all used it at the precise moment when we feel we are losing our balance, our feet are slipping out from under us, our hope is quickly diminishing, and the light at the end of the tunnel grows dim. And then, from somewhere deep inside our inner being, we grab hold of something that might give us a chance for overs, and we too muster up the courage to speak it to the world. "Hey, wait. This thing isn't over yet!"

Perhaps that is how you feel about your legacy: it leaves something to be desired. Basically, you feel that you've done a miserable job of leaving anything—material or otherwise—to your kids. If that is the case, then I ask you to pause and think of this:

- If you are still alive, you can change the course of your life.
- And if you are still breathing, you can change your legacy.

The reason you can change the trajectory of your life, and thus change your legacy, is because it's not over until God says it's over, and it's not the end until God says it's the end. And this is not the end, or you would already be dead and not reading this book.

It is not as important how we run the race as it is how we *finish* the race. And you, my friend, are still in this race called life.

I'm reminded of a familiar story from the book of Judges. In chapters 13–16, we find an amazing story of promise, failure, and victory—all about the same person. Samson was a child of promise, as the Lord had promised a son to Samson's mother before he was ever conceived. "For behold, you shall conceive and bear a son. And no razor shall come upon his head, for the child shall be a Nazarite to God from the womb; and he shall begin to deliver Israel out of the hands of the Philistines" (Judges 13:5). The boy Samson was to never cut his hair. The power of God would come upon him when he had hair, but if he cut his hair, the power of God would leave him. He lived his life this way, killing many of Israel's enemies by the power of God.

Trouble arose for Samson when he got involved with a harlot named Delilah. You probably know the story. The Philistines asked her to find out where Samson got his strength, yet Samson refused to tell

- *If you are still alive, you can change the course of your life.*
- *And if you are still breathing, you can change your legacy.*

Delilah the truth. Over and over, he told her lies about his strength, and each time, Samson broke free from the ropes she had used to tie him up. I guess the light bulb just never came on in Samson's head. Delilah eventually begged him to tell her the truth. In time, Samson's resistance wore thin and he told her that his strength was in his hair. The worst happened. While he was asleep, Delilah cut his hair. And just as God had said, when the Nazarite vow was broken, God's power departed.

This time, the Philistines were able to easily overpower Samson. "Then the Philistines took him and put out his eyes, and brought him down to Gaza. They bound him with bronze fetters, and he became a grinder in the prison" (Judges 16:21). Samson was the laughingstock of the town as they taunted and ridiculed him. Clearly, Samson's life was offtrack from what God had purposed for him. He was, by all accounts, a failure.

But don't forget that great line so eloquently stated by Yogi Berra. The truth remains that nothing is over until God says so. Even when we mess up royally, God always has a bigger and better plan than we can imagine.

In time, Samson's hair began to grow back, and while the slow process was taking place on his head, something of colossal worth was growing deep inside the heart of this man who was a Nazarite to God from birth. I believe in that dark, dingy, foul-smelling prison, Samson remembered who he was—who God designed him to be. I believe he knew where to turn when circumstances robbed him of his identity. I believe Samson turned to his God for help, and God heard that repentant, desperate cry from Samson's deeply wounded heart.

Haven't most of us been there—in a dark, dingy, foul-smelling prison of our own making? What about those circumstances that robbed us of our identity and we forgot who we were—who God had called us to be? Like Samson, we were blinded by the devastating results of bad behavior.

The apostle Paul nailed it when he wrote Romans 7. It seriously sounds like my own testimony. The Passion Translation so clearly depicts what is going on here.

> I'm a mystery to myself, for I want to do what is right, but end up doing what my moral instincts condemn … For I know that nothing good lives within the flesh of my fallen humanity. The longings to do what is right are within me, but will-power is not enough to accomplish it. My lofty desires to do what is good are dashed when I do the things I want to avoid. So if my behavior contradicts my desires to do good, I must conclude that it's not my true identity doing it, but the unwelcome intruder of sin hindering me from being who I really am. (Romans 7:15, 18–20 TPT)

Did you see the so-much-like-me statement at the beginning of that passage of scripture: "I'm a mystery to myself"? Or how about the part that says, "The longings to do what is right are within me, but willpower is not enough to accomplish it"? Still, the most gut-honest sentence I relate to is this: "I must conclude that it's not my true identity doing it."

Paul had lost his identity as the unwelcome intruder of sin kept him from being who he really was. I was stunned when I read this chapter a few days ago. Even the most amazing apostle of all times struggled with the very things we struggle with. Satan tries over and over to strip us of our identity in Christ. And on some days, I must admit that he seems to win.

But wait. This story isn't over yet!

One day, the Philistines were having a large celebration in honor of their pagan god, Dagon, giving him credit for the capture of Samson. In their excitement of worshipping Dagon, they decided to have Samson brought from prison so that he might perform for them. Obviously, this was designed only to make fun of him. Blind Samson was retrieved from prison and stationed between the pillars of the temple. He asked the lad who placed him there if he could lean against the pillars. The lad agreed. We could say that Samson *positioned* himself to be used in God's story!

When Samson was being watched by thousands of taunting Philistines—men and women alike—he called out to the Lord,

> "O Lord God, remember me, I pray! Strengthen me, I pray, just this once, O God, that I may with one blow take vengeance on the Philistines for my two eyes!" (Judges 16:28)

Having prayed that prayer,

> Samson took hold of the two middle pillars … and pushed with all his might, and the temple fell on the lords and all the people who were in it. So the dead that he killed at his death were more than he had killed in his life. (Judges 16:29–30)

What if Samson hadn't responded to God's last tug at his heart—to remember who he was and his calling in life? If he hadn't, that greatest victory of all (killing more of God's enemies in this one last effort than in his whole life put together) would not have happened. Samson would be left with only his terrible mistakes and bad choices as a legacy. But that is *not* what happened!

Samson took a chance of letting God use him one more time, and this time, Samson got it right. He became a participant in God's great story to rescue His people—Israel—and bring glory to His name. Think about this: Samson made it into the great "Heroes of Faith" in Hebrews 11. Samson had the final say as to what his earthly story would tell us thousands of years later, and he clearly falls into the category of *heroes*—not failures!

It doesn't matter how terrible our mistakes and bad our choices are. We are never too far gone for God to rescue us. We are never too far out of our Father's reach. We are never too sin-stained that He won't forgive. We are never too hopeless for God to welcome His children back home—where we belong.

Do terrible mistakes and bad choices sound familiar to you? They do to me. Or perhaps what we have are some of those not-so-terrible mistakes and not-so-bad choices, but they are not-so-perfect either. You know how it goes. A little yielding here, a compromise there, doing my own thing, a step away from who I knew God called me to be. In that compromised position, we waste our hours, days, weeks, months, and even years away from God's plan for our lives.

Paul asked the Christians in the church at Rome, "So tell me, what benefit ensued from doing those things that you're now ashamed of? It left you with nothing but a legacy of shame and death" (Romans 6:21 TPT).

Could it be that Romans 6:21 describes our legacy—a legacy that we are ashamed of? So how might we remedy that not-so-good legacy of ours? One thing we cannot do is change the past. It has come and gone. But we can change today, the here and now. If we still have breath,

*We are never too hopeless for God to welcome His children back home—where we belong.*

we can change our trajectory—even at this late hour. Paul did. Remember that he was credited with trying to stamp out Christianity by persecuting and killing Christians? He had a not-so-good past, wouldn't you agree? Yet when Paul was converted to Christianity on the road to Damascus, he did an about-face. He later wrote in Philippians 3:13, "But one thing I do, forgetting those things which are behind and reaching forward to those things which are ahead." We can do it too! We can have the power to finish differently from how it seems right now, if we will accept God's offer of the greatest exchange of all time—our faith for His righteousness.

## Meanwhile, Back in Texas

At the time of the Bode family tragedy, Hallis Parker was the only one of Oscar and Ethel's children who was serving the Lord. They had all grown up in a Christian family, sung the gospel songs, and attended many church services. Their lives were shaped by their childhood environment, yet somewhere along the way, they made some of those not-so-terrible mistakes and not-so-bad choices. I don't know for certain about any of their wrong turns—since as a child I thought they were perfect—but I do know what happened with each one of them in the end.

## Floy Bode

Uncle Floy was a busy businessman. There were long days operating a gasoline station, feed business, TV repairs, being veterinarian for the community, and board meetings galore. For most of those years, there was such a thing as blue laws in Texas, and businesses could not actually be open on Sunday. Blue laws were intended to forbid the sale of certain items on Sundays so owners and employees go to church and rest. Floy didn't go to church, nor did he rest. I suspect that if he could have been open on Sundays, he would have seen a reason to be—just for the sake of all those who needed something from him. Rest wasn't included in his mode of operation.

That is, until he suffered a stroke. There he lay, flat on his back in the hospital in Fredericksburg, Texas, unable to talk. When something like this happens, one has plenty of time to rest and think. It wasn't a question of whether or not Floy believed in God, because he did. His upbringing had shaped the man he was, but his busy lifestyle had claimed him. God was not important. Well, until now.

As the days in the hospital slowly passed by, Floy began to move his arms and legs again, yet his speech did not improve. For three grueling days, he could not speak a word. How does one run a business or two, chair important boards, or tend to a thousand issues a day if one can't talk? This was serious business to Floy as he lay there staring at the ceiling. What would happen if he never spoke again? Had he taught his son enough that he could take over the businesses? Would he have to resign from the boards and his duties with the Harper Cemetery? The what-ifs filled his mind, and more importantly, worry filled his heart.

Perhaps it was time to give God some of his time. Doesn't that sound just like us? When things are good, we don't have enough time to give any to God. Then we find ourselves slamming into a brick wall, and *bam!* We suddenly have time for God! Nothing but time—flat on our backs, just counting time. I've been there, and the chances are that you have too. That is precisely where Floy Bode—the oldest son, the large-and-in-charge son, the one who could juggle multiple agendas—was at this moment in time. I'm confident there wasn't anything humorous about any of this, but I somehow catch a glimpse of our Heavenly Father peering down from heaven to see if my uncle has any time for Him now.

Perhaps you and I have never done what Floy did next. He bargained with God. Since the words couldn't be uttered, he spoke with his heart. It went something like this: "God, if You will give me back my health and my voice, I will give You my heart and my life."

In a few weeks, Floy's health improved, his voice came back, and he returned to work. But he didn't forget his bargain with God. It looked as if on the Sunday morning he planned to be at church he also had a conflicting commitment. He spoke to his brother-in-law, the pastor of the church. Uncle Carlos asked him, "What's wrong with tonight? It's Wednesday and we're having church."

Floy went to church that night, and he kept his commitment to the Lord. Right there in front of God and the whole church on August 12, 1973, Floy surrendered his heart and life to God. Two weeks later, he was baptized by that same brother-in-law. For the remainder of his life, Uncle Floy sat in the pew beside his wife and children every time the church doors were opened. It wasn't unusual for Floy to stand up and give a testimony of what great things God had done for him. He often shared a great truth he had learned through this trial—one truth he would never forget: "Don't take time to be holy. *Make* time to be holy." Clearly, this oldest son of Oscar and Ethel Bode had come home.

In his later years, Floy struggled with lung cancer. He had surgery to remove most of one lung. A year later, the cancer was back. His wife and son were the main caregivers, with daughter Elaine coming as often as she could. The last trip she made to see her dad was not at all what she expected. She never imagined the scene that was about to unfold before her eyes. This beloved daughter was the very reason Floy was still clinging to life. As the last member of the family to assure him it was all right to leave, Elaine held his head in her arms and said, "Dad, it is okay to go. Just wait for me by the gate." Father and daughter had their moment—one that ties them together until they meet again. Floy took two final breaths and passed over to the other side.

## Cecil Bode

My dad was as honest a man who ever lived. Nobody could have made him cheat anyone—ever. He worked hard his entire life, paying his own way and never looking for or accepting a handout. He was a private man who lived a quiet and peaceable life, minding his own business. When I was a child, he wanted my mother, sister, and me to go to church. He and my brother only went on rare occasions, such as when some of our Texas relatives were visiting us. However, my dad made a habit of watching his favorite television preacher, Rev. Rex Humbard, every Sunday morning at the Cathedral of Tomorrow. Humbard was a spirited Pentecostal preacher who nearly scared me to death. But my mom and dad both loved him, and when he finished each Sunday, I felt like I had been to church. My dad never spoke of a time that he had accepted Christ as his Savior, and none of us ever asked him.

Many years later, when my dad was in his sixties, he moved from Oklahoma back to his hometown of Harper, Texas. There he and my stepmother, Esther, attended the church that my family had helped establish in the 1930s. The church was holding a revival, and apparently my dad liked the preacher because he went several nights in a row. He was especially drawn to the music—and the music was always good. The singing Besch Family with Merlene Besch at the piano could stir anyone's dry, parched soul. My dad loved David, Merlene, and their four children. Also, for as long as I can remember, my cousins sang as a quartet. It included Carolyn and her husband, Levi Ellebracht, Buzzy singing bass (and playing the bass fiddle), and Zane's husband, Chester Deiter. For most of their adult lives, they sang at church every Sunday, as well as many community events. A special treat always happened for me when I visited their church and was invited to sing with them.

On Sunday afternoon at the end of the revival, there was a baptismal service at the Little Devil's River on Uncle Carlos's ranch. My brother, sister-in-law, and niece were being baptized as a family that day. Dad had gone to that baptismal service as a spectator—so everyone thought. He had not spoken to anyone about his decision, yet when all the candidates had been baptized, he took off his cowboy boots, handed his hat and billfold to my stepmother, and waded into the water. Dad was baptized that day, and in one awe-filled moment in time, he returned to the God of his parents. If heaven's residents could have seen that event happening on earth, I'm certain my grandparents were rejoicing that another son had come home.

I never talked to Dad about his baptism; I just know how he lived out the remainder of his days. He had always been a believer, and that was confirmed a few years ago when a family friend published an article in the *Atoka County Times,* in Atoka, Oklahoma. Although my dad passed away in 1988, in the year 2014, Robert "Tot" Calvert wrote the article honoring my parents titled "In Memory of a Very Special Couple." He ended the article with these words: "Cecil also believed in a Supreme Being and told me so. He was the most-polite man I ever worked for."[2]

Until the day of my dad's funeral, I had no idea that he had helped an individual who had been released from prison. A bright, young man came up to me, introduced himself, and told me that my dad had made it financially possible for him to attend a Bible College. The young man was so grateful, and he wanted us to know what our dad had done for him behind the scenes.

Whatever my dad did or didn't do with his life, I know that he got the ending right. Since childhood, he had heard Jesus call, "Come, follow me" (Matthew 4:19 NIV). And on this day, right there in the middle of Little Devil's River, my dad accepted that call and settled the matter of where he would spend eternity.

## LaVerne (Nonnie) Parker

The youngest daughter of Oscar and Ethel would recover slowly from the tragedy. During the earlier years, she was under a doctor's care—going to the doctor one or two times per week. She avoided people and gatherings and tried intently to hide it all from her daughter. Yet Carolyn remembered those years very well as they had brought much pain to her own life. During one conversation with her, Carolyn told me, "My mother was so sick I thought she was going to die."

While Nonnie's condition was gradually improving, she suffered a setback when her sister-in-law died from cancer. Following that event, her father-in-law, Tommy Parker, committed suicide. Carolyn would lose yet another grandparent. Each setback took another huge toll on Nonnie's health, yet each time, she would start again. A breakthrough came for her when she turned to the God of her parents. With the Lord's help, she found her way to recovery, taking one tiny step at a time.

However, God doesn't waste one thing. The slow and grueling process to wholeness built an unshakable foundation of faith that would sustain my aunt for the remainder of her life. She became a pillar in the church and an amazing wife and mother and was adored by some nieces who thought she was the sweetest person on earth. She also spent a lifetime praying for her husband, J.H. (Son) Parker, to come to Christ. It would take many years of believing God for an answer to that prayer.

Today, many of God's children are still out there—away from their Heavenly Father and away from their true identity. They need to come home. Are you one of them? Has life dealt you some cards that didn't play out so well and as a result you lost your way? The years have been stained with terrible decisions and bad choices, leaving you with a legacy of shame. Perhaps you even blame God for it all.

If any of those words ring true in your heart, please know that it is not too late for you to turn to the Heavenly Father. His amazing grace—*unmerited favor*—awaits you. The words of the song "Amazing Grace" resemble my own testimony. Maybe it's your testimony as well. I rejoice at the oh-so-familiar words. Verse after verse, songwriter John Newton defined me accurately.

## Amazing Grace

Amazing grace, how sweet the sound
That saved a wretch like me
I once was lost, but now am found
T'was blind but now I see.

T'was grace that taught my heart to fear
And grace, my fears relieved
How precious did that grace appear
The hour I first believed.

Through many dangers, toils and snares
We have already come
T'was grace that brought us safe thus far
And grace will lead us home.[3]

It is God's great grace that will wipe the slate clean, taking away our yesterdays, our mistakes, and our lostness. And it is that same grace-gift that will give us a new pathway for today and all of our tomorrows. And then, at the end of our time on earth, grace will lead us home.

Uncle Son ran from God for ninety-three years, but in the final week of his life, he called out to the Lord to save him. My aunt's prayers were answered as Uncle Son found mercy and grace just days before he died. With a million-dollar-size smile on his face, he gave a glorious testimony that God is indeed a loving and forgiving God.

In the end, they all came home.

With God, it's not over until you win![4] —Marilyn Hickey

CHAPTER FOURTEEN

# THE CONCLUSION

The days following my husband's funeral were shaky for me as I searched for truth. Life and death were warring inside my heart. It seemed so final. So over. So unfair. Reality was staring me in the face as never before. The words struck a chord when my five-year-old grandson asked, "Why did Pawpaw get to go to heaven first?"

I had to process the phrase "get to go" for a minute, wondering how I would answer his question. I quickly surveyed the pain I had endured over the past few months, and from that viewpoint, it certainly seemed as though *getting to go* was the privileged position. In that one brief moment of time, God used a five-year-old child to cast his grandfather's death from a totally different perspective—one that I would never forget. Holding back my tears, I finally answered Braden. "God has left me here because He knows that you, your baby sister, Katie, and your soon-to-be-born first cousin, Landon, all need Grannie to help them grow up."

In this modern age of Christianity, the walk of faith has been greatly misunderstood. It is not now, nor has it ever been, a magic formula for a carefree life. We will never understand our journey with God if we try to put it into our terms. The Bible tells us, "Lean not on your own understanding" (Proverbs 3:5). God knew our natural, finite minds could not handle such difficult things, so it is by faith that we can trust in a God who can. I will trust Him because I can trust Him, for He is trustworthy!

And it is by that same faith we can walk into the recovery God has for us—the healing of our wounded souls.

I began to understand that my grief was all about me. It had nothing to do with my departed husband. He had arrived. He was free. He was with Jesus! I was basically sad for *me*. It was the huge hole in my heart that caused me to mourn. Oh, how accurate my glimpse of truth just a few days before: Pawpaw *got to go* first. That is indeed the privileged position, and it is the ones left behind who are suffering and sorrowful. Our mourning is for us, not our departed loved ones, for no one is ever disappointed when they reach that awesome place called heaven.

A few months later, I heard a song that so clearly said in words what I was feeling in my heart. Songwriter Gloria Gaither must surely have known this very revelation as she wrote "It's Not about Now."[1] In her goal to comfort those who hear this song, she points us to another place, a place not *here*, but *there*. Yet because we haven't been *there*, we are skeptics, and we actually like *here* better. Nonetheless, I think we are

> *We will never understand our journey with God if we try to put it into our terms.*

entirely too earthly minded since we are clearly told, "Set your mind on things above, not on things on the earth" (Colossians 3:2).

The apostle Paul wrote a stirring letter to the Christians at the church in Corinth. His words certainly spoke of hope and encouragement to these persecuted Christians, but it also spoke about where Paul was in his own painful, earthly journey. Listen for the longing in Paul's words for his new home in heaven, but also hear the even deeper yearning of his heart to accept whatever God chooses for him. The Message version of 2 Corinthians 5:1–9 is incredible.

> For instance, we know that when these bodies of ours are taken down like tents and folded away, they will be replaced by resurrection bodies in heaven—God-made, not handmade—and we'll never have to relocate our "tents" again. Sometimes we can hardly wait to move—and so we cry out in frustration. Compared to what's

coming, living conditions around here seem like a stopover in an unfurnished shack, and we're tired of it! We've been given a glimpse of the real thing, our true home, our resurrection bodies! The Spirit of God whets our appetite by giving us a taste of what's ahead. He puts a little of heaven in our hearts so that we'll never settle for less. That's why we live with such good cheer. You won't see us drooping our heads or dragging our feet! Cramped conditions here don't get us down. They only remind us of the spacious living conditions ahead. It's what we trust in but don't yet see that keeps us going. Do you suppose a few ruts in the road or rocks in the path are going to stop us? When the time comes, we'll be plenty ready to exchange exile for homecoming. But neither exile nor homecoming is the main thing. Cheerfully pleasing God is the main thing, and that's what we aim to do, regardless of our conditions. (2 Corinthians 5:1–9 MSG)

During my entire recovery, my son, Brent, encouraged me to "think eternal," a concept from *The Purpose Driven Life*. Rick Warren's wisdom helped me embrace a new perspective about my life now.

I truly wanted to *think eternal* as I lived the rest of my time on earth and especially as I faced an unknown future. With God's help, I began to view earth as the prelude to heaven and grasp the fact that life counts only when it lines up with eternal values. I continually had to ask myself these questions: "Does my prelude match the music to come? Is it appropriately announcing and leading into the song of heaven?"

> *Death is not the end. Death is the transition to the real music, and the real music is heaven.*

A prelude is only a sample of what is to come, and so is our earthly life. The two—earthly and eternal—are connected. Why can't we see that? Why are we so focused on *here and now* instead of *there and then?* The best part is just ahead of us. Our loved ones didn't have to go first; they got to go first. Death is not the end. Death is the transition to the real music, and the real music is heaven.

If we can receive it, Oscar, Ethel, and Leo *got to go* first.

In the end, it is God's story.

And in the end, we win!

> To make the most of your life, you must keep the vision of eternity continually in your mind and the value of it in your heart. There's far more to life than just here and now![2] —Rick Warren

APPENDIX A: THE HISTORY:
THE LONG VERSION

———

## History Matters

It is our family story that most clearly defines who we are as a people—rich
or poor, strong or weak, proud or humble, good or not-so-good, religious
or nonreligious—all characteristics that describe our group, those people
called by our last name. My dad's family surname is *Bode*, a German name
for which we have known roots in the nation of Germany as far back as
the mid-1800s.

Many Germans came to America during the early colonial years for
various reasons—one being the advantage of free land as German religious
groups were being suppressed by their government just as those in England.
Those who came to America thought relocation to a new land to be the
only solution. By the time of the American Revolution, nearly 200,000
Germans had settled in New England states—mainly Pennsylvania. These
were called the "Pennsylvania Dutch." Later, in the middle of the 1800s,
another group of immigrants from Germany made their way to the shores
of America, settling in the Midwest. They had left Germany because of
political turmoil and agricultural failures. It is believed there were as many
as 1.5 million Germans who came during that era, of which my ancestors
were a part.[1]

## The Bode Family Roots

Many families from Germany settled in what is known today as the Texas Hill
Country, making up a large part of the pioneer population of the area. The

———

earliest Bode who migrated to America was a young man named Carl Bode. It is believed that Carl wrote to his family back in Germany reporting that Texas was a good place to settle and pointing out the route they should take to join him. In 1855, my great-great-grandfather, Robert Bode, a brother to Carl, migrated to the United States from Germany. In 1853, Robert married Johanna Radetzky, and their oldest son, Carl Johann Robert Bode, was born in 1854 while still in Germany. It would be the following year that the young couple and their infant son set sail for the southern shores of the United States. They were accompanied by Robert's parents, Carl and Charlotte (Weisse) Bode, and one sister, Agnes, and her husband, Otto Lange.[2]

For six long weeks this group was on the water looking anxiously for the new land of which they had heard. On July 26, 1855, they landed at Indianola, a small harbor about thirty miles due south of Victoria, Texas. Among the possessions that they brought with them were two iron wheel wagons. At Indianola they bought a yoke of oxen and started out in search for their new home in the adopted land.[3]

The growing family moved several times, eventually settling north of Castell in Mason County near the mountains later known as Bode Peaks. After a short period, they moved to Cold Creek in Llano County. In 1872, the family returned to Mason County, about eight miles northwest of Castell, and established their final home. Their children married and began families of their own, and for fifteen years, all of the Robert Bode family lived within a four-mile radius of one another. The settlement was called Bodeville, although few, if any, family members currently live there.[4]

One of the ten additional children born to Robert and Johanna after arriving in the United States was my great-grandfather, Paul Otto Bode, in 1865. For many generations, the Bode family made their living by farming and ranching. Like most folks in those days, they had strong work ethics coupled with strong faith in God. It took both to survive the hardships of life in unchartered territory. The Bodes were Methodist, being converts of the Martin Luther Reformation era.

In 1889, Paul Otto Bode married my great-grandmother, Anna Radetzky. Anna would be the second Radetzky to marry into the Bode family, the first being Johanna Radetzky, who had married Robert Bode. The Radetzky family dates back as far as the eleventh century and has a colorful history to say the least.

# The Radetzky Family Roots

The Radetzky family descended from an ancient Czech (Bohemian) family of nobility. Their castle was situated in the county of Bidschow and was destroyed in the Hussite wars. The first Radetzky who has been documentarily traced is Johann Radetzky von Radetz and Tarnow. He received confirmation of his nobility and coat of arms from the king of Bohemia in 1329. He was recognized for his valiant and loyal service, perhaps in the Mongolian wars, by Johann's ancestors.

The descendants of Johann were Probislow Radetzky, the founder of the church at Chomutitz in the fourteenth century, likely a Hussite church, as the Radetzkys were Hussites. Also, Wenzel Radetzky, who had the inheritance from his father, entered in the patent records as "Maierhof and Village of Radetz" in 1545, as well as his part in the villages of Chomutitz and Newralitz.

The later counts Radetzky von Radetz date their line of nobility from Knight Adam Heinrich Radetzky and his wife, Elizabeth Xopska von Zapa, who lived around 1600. His sons took the title of count.

Johann Georg Radetzky was made a baron by Emperor Leopold I in 1684 and was a royal captain in Bohemia. Wenzel Leopold Radetzky was royal chamberlain and made a count by Empress Maria Theresa in 1764. Peter Eusebius Radetzky's wife, Baroness Maria Veronica Bechenin von Lazan, was a Roman Catholic; therefore, Peter became a loyal Roman Catholic.

Count Peter Eusebius Radetzky's son, Joseph Wenzel Anton Radetzky, is worthy of honorable mention. He became a noted field marshal in the Austrian army. He was born in Bohemia in 1766 and married Countess Franciska Strassolde in 1797. Together they had five sons and three daughters; only one son, Theodor, and one daughter, Franciska, grew to adulthood.[5]

Joseph (also spelled Josef) was a Bohemian nobleman and Austrian Field Marshal. He served as chief of the general staff in the Habsburg Monarchy during the later period of the Napoleonic Wars and afterwards began military reforms. Radetzky is best known for the victories at the Battles of Custoza (24–25 July 1848) and Novara (23 March 1849) during the First Italian War of Independence … After his triumph in Italy, he was made Viceroy of Lombardy-Venetia from 1848 to 1857 … He also commanded the Austrian troops who reconquered Venice after the year-long siege of the rebellious city in May 1848–August 1849. He became a Knight of the Order of the Golden Fleece in 1848.[6]

He retired at age ninety and was immortalized by Johann Strauss I's "Radetzky March." The march became an unofficial Austrian national anthem. Today, it is a national treasure and is played at the finale of every concert by the Vienna Philharmonic as well major sports events, in particular at football matches of the Austrian national team. It is also a well-loved piece of classical music for young learners.[7]

The first memorial of Radetzky was built in Prague. It was planned during his life, since the Battle of Novara in 1849. It was first designed in 1851 by the painter Christian Ruben and later sculpted by brothers Emanuel Max (statue of Radetzky) and Josef Max (statues of soldiers). However, the memorial was unveiled several months after Radetzky's death, on November 13, 1858. It was regarded as one of the most beautiful memorials in Prague. Radetzky was popular among the Czech people as a great compatriot. The statue is now exhibited in the Lapidarium of Czech National Museum.[8]

The wars and persecutions following the Reformation caused many of the Czechs, who held to the doctrine of Huss and Hyronimus, to leave Bohemia (Austria) about the year 1780. King Frederick II (Frederick the Great) of Prussia invited the persecuted Protestants to make their home in Prussia.[9]

Among those who left Bohemia (Austria) and moved to Prussia were Joseph Wenzel Radetzky, Georg Radetzky, and Christian Radetzky, along with many others in approximately 1780. It is not clear if these three were brothers or cousins to the notable field marshal, but they were near relatives. All three lost their title of nobility when they migrated to Prussia.[10]

The above Georg Radetzky settled in Leubusch, Kreis (County) of Brieg in the province of Silesia and is my ancestor. His descendants are Georg Frederick Radetzky, who remained in Germany, and Georg Radetzky, who was born in Leubusch in October 1815 and also remained in Germany. The later Georg Radetzky had sons, William, Carl, Johann, and George, and one daughter, Caroline. Of these children, both William, born in 1838, and George, born in 1851, migrated to the United States.[11]

The above-mentioned William married Susanna Radetzky (a relative and daughter of Frederick Radetzky) in 1865. The couple had six children, three of whom died in infancy. The other three children were daughters, Marie and Anna, and son, Frederick William, who migrated from Prussia with their parents and settled in Bodeville, Texas, in May 1884. Anna was eleven years old.

Bodeville is where my great-grandparents, Paul Otto Bode and Anna Radetzky, were married on January 2, 1889. Paul and Anna Bode had a total of twelve children, three of whom died in infancy. Their oldest son was my grandfather Oscar Robert Bode, who was born in October 1889. He was followed by siblings Selma (Bode) McDonald, Aurora (Bode) Barker, Reseda (Bode) Walker, Reuben Bode, Elgin Bode, Milton "Bill" Bode, Forrest Bode, and Clifford Bode.[12]

Throughout my childhood years, I knew and loved many of these relatives and played with their children and grandchildren. The annual Paul and Anna Bode reunion made that possible. I also remember going to the home of Clifford Bode to visit my elderly great-grandmother, Anna, in the 1960s. At that young age, I was clueless about her rich history spanning two continents. I can only hope that someone captured her story before she left this earth in 1966, but if they did, I do not know about it.

These great-grandparents moved to Harper, Texas, a small town in Gillespie County, in 1901. There my grandfather, Oscar Robert Bode, met my grandmother, Ethel Iva McDonald. They were married on August 6, 1908. Ethel was the daughter of William Augustus McDonald and Louanna Elizabeth (Lacy) McDonald, who are my maternal great-grandparents and have fascinating family histories.

## The McDonald Family Roots

The McDonalds migrated to Texas from Illinois and were among the earliest pioneers who came to the Hill Country of Texas. As early as the 1850s, the McDonald frontiersmen helped establish various settlements, including Harper, as well as an area west of Fredericksburg, a well-known and visited German-style town and tourist attraction today. One popular tourist site located in Fredericksburg's backyard is the Willow City Loop with its spectacular fields of bluebonnets—the state flower of Texas.

Pioneers Eli McDonald and his wife, Caroline, and their children were part of the tragedy that occurred in August 1864, in which Eli lost his life. His wife and five children were taken captive and held for many months. Their story is one of hardships and suffering. Caroline McDonald and the five children, two of whom were her daughters, were discovered on a reservation at Fort Sill. Caroline managed to give some kind of signal to a visitor, who later reported the information to government officials. Her brave action resulted in their release not long afterward.

Today, the sight known as the McDonald Massacre is officially marked by a Texas Historical Marker on the east side of Harper. These early settlers lived in constant fear and several lost their lives protecting their families, homes, and livestock. A description of those early days is documented in a book titled *Here's Harper*, published in 1963. The book was assembled by the Harper Centennial Committee to commemorate the one hundredth anniversary of the town of Harper, Texas, from 1863 to 1963.

Another story of tragedy that occurred in the McDonald family was that of Lafe McDonald's wife, Alwilda, and her mother, Mrs. Wiley Joy, who lost their lives at Banta Branch. No doubt, life on the Texas frontier was filled with adversity, fears, and yes, tragedy.[13]

## The Lacy (Lacey) Family Roots

My maternal great-grandmother's family was named Lacy. Her family history traces back to that of William Lacy and Elliott Lacy, based on the research of Hubert Wesley Lacey.

The descendants of William Lacy stretch from Georgia to Texas and include a Miss America, Mary Ann Mobley, from Mississippi in 1958. Drury Lacy, son of William, founded a dynasty, and was vice president of Hampden-Sydney College, where many of his offspring received their education. They became doctors, ministers, missionaries, soldiers, and politicians. Drury Lacy Jr. was one of the founders of Davidson College. Another son, William Sterling Lacy, was a well-known minister and was called the "sweet singer in Israel." William's grandson, Dr. Benjamin Rice Lacy, was president of Union Theological Seminary. Four of his sons served in the Civil War. One, Major James Horace Lacy, was a high-ranking officer. Another, Rev. Beverly Tucker Lacy, was a personal minister to Gen. Stonewall Jackson and was with him on that fateful night when he was mortally wounded by his own men. There is a picture (in their family book) of Rev. Lacy and Gen. Jackson kneeling in prayer and a picture of the marker where Rev. Lacy buried Stonewall's amputated arm at Ellwood, the Lacy Plantation.

Elliott Lacy and his son, Elliott Jr., were both killed in the Revolutionary War. Elliott's descendants spread across the Midwest to Texas to California and beyond. Lionel Primm Lacey was a lawyer who opposed Abe Lincoln in court on several occasions. During the war, there were Lacys who fought on both sides and several instances in this family where brothers served on different sides, including at least one battle in which brothers fought each other with deadly consequences. In some cases, they switched sides.[14]

There were law men and outlaws, con men and cons, Texas Rangers and enemy fighters. Lacys have served their country in every major war from the Revolutionary War to Vietnam, some making the supreme sacrifice. They were officers and enlisted men, army, navy, air force and marines. The Lacy women were missionaries, doctors, teachers, and homemakers. Pioneer women worked beside their husbands, and in some cases raised large families, too.[15]

We must never forget that history matters.

# ENDNOTES

## Introduction

1   William T. Sleeper, "Jesus, I Come," 1887, public domain.

## Chapter 1 – The Tragedy

1   "Triple Funeral Services Were Held Here Saturday," *Fredericksburg Standard,* July 3, 1946, Fredericksburg, Texas, 9.

2   "Harper Family of 3 Discovered Dead on Ranch," *The Austin American,* June 28, 1946, Austin, Texas, 1.

3   "Officers Seek Clue to Triple Tragedy," *Valley Morning Star,* June 29, 1946, Harlingen, Texas, 1.

4   "Farm Family Is Shot to Death," the *Waco News-Tribune,* June 29, 1946, Waco, Texas, 1.

5   "Harper Mourns Tragic Death of Bodes in Triple Slaying," *Fredericksburg Standard,* July 3, 1946, Fredericksburg, Texas, 9.

6   "Three Members of Family Found Shot," *Lubbock Evening Journal,* June 28, 1946, Lubbock, Texas, 15.

7   "Triple Funeral Services Were Held Here Saturday," *Fredericksburg Standard,* July 3, 1946, Fredericksburg, Texas, 9.

8   "Funeral Services Held for Bode Family Saturday," *Kerrville Mountain Sun,* July 4, 1946, Kerrville, Texas, 1.

9   Ann Voskamp, *The Way of Abundance* (Grand Rapids, Michigan: Zondervan, 2018), 23; John 9:3 MSG.

10  Ibid., 23; John 9:3 (NLT).

11  Ibid., 23.

12  Charles Spurgeon, *Morning and Evening,* Updated Language Edition (Grand Rapids, Michigan: Discovery House, 2016) p. 381, from the July 5 reading.

## Chapter 2 – The Gathering

1    Bobby Richardson, accessed June 25, 2020, quoted at https://pastorterryblog. wordpress. com /2010/02/28/sunday-sermon-your-will-nothing-more-nothing-less-nothing-else.

## Chapter 3 – The History

1    Beatrice Bayley, "History of Ethnic Origins," *Family Heritage Book* (Beatrice Bayley, Inc. Publisher). Additional reference: accessed on June 25, 2020, https:// en.wikipedia.org/wiki/German _Americans #Texas.

2    Sadie Olene (Barrett) Walker and Karen Eileen (Barrett) Craig Lerma, *The Bode and Radetzky Families History*, unpublished manuscripts. Used by permission.

3    Ibid.

4    Accessed June 24, 2020, https://en.wikipedia.org/wiki/Radetzky_March 5.

5    Sadie Olene (Barrett) Walker and Karen Eileen (Barrett) Craig Lerma, *The Bode and Radetzky Families History*, unpublished manuscripts. Used by permission.

6    Centennial Committee, *Here's Harper* (Fredericksburg, Texas: The Radio Post, Inc. 1963), 3–5, 15, 47, 63.

7    Hubert Wesley and Howard Elton Lacey, *The William Lacy and Elliott Lacy Families of New Kent and Chesterfield Counties, Virginia* (Chelsea, Michigan: BookCrafters, 1996), vol. 1, no. 5.

8    Steve Green and Jon Mohr, "Find Us Faithful," published by Birdwing Music (ASCAP) and Jonathan Mark Music (ASCAP), 1987.

9    Priscilla Shirer, *Awaken* (Nashville, Tennessee: B&H Publishing Group, 2017), 208.

## Chapter 4 – The Family I Knew

1    Gene Bode, *If the Bench Could Talk: Fifty Years at Bode's*, self-published, 4.

2    Doug Perkins, "A Delicate Balance," *The Cattleman Magazine*, September 1980, 47–50.

3    Gene Bode, *If the Bench Could Talk: Fifty Years at Bode's*, self-published, 84–85.

4    Ibid., 88.

5    Oswald Chambers, *My Utmost for His Highest*, special updated edition (Grand Rapids, Michigan: Discovery House Publishers, 1995) from the March 19 reading; accessed June 25, 2020, https://utmost.org/abraham%E2%80%99s-life-of-faith/.

## Chapter 5 – The Grandparents I Never Knew

1   Gene Bode, *If the Bench Could Talk*: *Fifty Years at Bode's*, self-published, 1.
2   Hallis (Bode) Parker, *History Lighthouse Fellowship Chapel*, March 25, 2006, Harper, Texas.
3   Bill Guild, "Have You Seen," *History Lighthouse Fellowship Chapel*, March 25, 2006, Harper, Texas.
4   Hallis (Bode) Parker, *History Lighthouse Fellowship Chapel*, March 25, 2006, Harper, Texas, n.p.
5   Gene Bode, *If the Bench Could Talk: Fifty Years at Bode's,* self-published, 14.1-14.2.
6   Andrew Murray, quoted by Louis Parkhurst Jr., *The Believer's Secret of the Abiding Presence* (Minneapolis, Minnesota: Bethany House Publishers, 1987), 120.

## Chapter 6 – The Aftermath

1   Genesis 6:8.
2   James 4:6.
3   1 Corinthians 15:10.
4   John 1:16.
5   John 1:14.
6   Acts 4:33.
7   Romans 5:20.
8   2 Corinthians 12:9.
9   Ephesians 2:8–9.
10  Hebrews 4:16.
11  Annie Johnson Flint, "He Giveth More Grace" © 1941, Renewed 1969 Lillenas Publishing Co., *The Baptist Hymnal* (Nashville, Tennessee: Lifeway Worship, ©2008), 113.
12  Amy Carmichael, quoted by David Hazard, *You Are My Hiding Place* (Minneapolis, Minnesota: Bethany House Publisher, 1991), 96.

## Chapter 7 – The Survivors

1   Amy Carmichael, quoted by David Hazard, *You Are My Hiding Place* (Minneapolis, Minnesota: Bethany House Publisher, 1991), 70.
2   *Macmillan Dictionary,* accessed June 25, 2020, https://www.macmillandictionary.com/ us/dictionary/american/lose-your-bearings.
3   Ann Voskamp, *The Way of Abundance* (Grand Rapids, Michigan: Zondervan, 2018), 24.

4  G. A. Young, "God Lead Us Along," public domain.

5  Robert Browning, accessed June 25, 2020, https://en.wikisource.org/wiki/Ixion_ (Browning).

## Chapter 8 – The Purpose

1  Rick Warren, *The Purpose Driven Life* (Grand Rapids, Michigan: Zondervan, 2002), 18.

2  Matt Redman (Jason Ingram, Matt Redman, Tim Wanstall), "Never Once," *10,000 Reasons* album, Capitol CMG Publishing, 2011.

3  Ann Voskamp, *The Way of Abundance* (Grand Rapids, Michigan: Zondervan, 2018), 22.

4  Ibid., 158.

5  Henri Nouwen, *The Return of the Prodigal Son* (New York, New York: Doubleday, 1992).

6  Ibid., 106.

7  Chris Tiegreen, *The One Year at His Feet Devotional* (Atlanta, Georgia: Tyndale House Publishers, 2003) from the June 8 reading.

8  Rick Warren, *The Purpose Driven Life* (Grand Rapids, Michigan: Zondervan, 2002), 231.

9  Ibid., 233.

10 Darrell Scott, accessed June 20, 2020, quoted from https://www.cpr.org/2018/02/22/darrell-scott-father-of-a-columbine-victim-calls-for-culture-of-connectedness/.

11 Rev. Porter, accessed June 20, 2020, quoted from https://en.wikipedia.org/wiki/Rachel_Scott.

12 Gloria Gaither, *Heaven* (Nashville, Tennessee: J. Countryman, a division of Thomas Nelson, Inc., 2003, Cover.

13 Oswald Chambers, *My Utmost for His Highest* (Grand Rapids, Michigan: Discovery House Publishers, 1995) from the May 22 reading.

14 Miriam Huffman Rockness, *Images of Faith* (Mt. Dora, Florida: Lilias Trotter Legacy, Inc. 2019), 67.

## Chapter 9 – The Wounds

1  Daniel Gardner, "My Life Is in You, Lord," ©1986, Integrity's Hosanna! Music (ASCAP), Baptist Hymnal (Nashville, Tennessee: Baptist Hymnal, 2008), 518.

2  Lilias Trotter, *A Way of Seeing: The Inward and Outward Vision of Lilias Trotter* (Coppell, Texas: Lilias Trotter Legacy, Inc. 2020), 62.

## Chapter 10 – The Triumph

1   Bret Baier, "A Life That Matters," documentary, Fox News Channel, October 25, 2013, from https://www.charleskrauthammer.com/documentarymedia; accessed June 20, 2020.

2   Priscilla Shirer, *Awaken* (Nashville, Tennessee: B&H Publishing Group, 2017), 256.

3   Sheila Walsh, *It's Okay Not to be Okay* (Grand Rapids, Michigan: Baker Books, a division of Baker Publishing Group, 2018), 140.

4   Used by permission.

5   Amy Carmichael, *Whispers of His Power* (Fort Washington, Pennsylvania: CLC Publications, 1982), 146, from the July 5 reading.

6   Oswald Chambers, *My Utmost for His Highest* (Grand Rapids, Michigan: Discovery House Publishers, 1995) from the August 2, reading.

7   Winnie the Pooh, https://bayart.org/winnie-the-pooh-quotes.

8   Amy Carmichael, quoted by Elizabeth Elliott, *A Chance to Die* (Grand Rapids, Michigan: Revell, 1987), 367.

9   Charles Krauthammer, quoted by Richard M. Langworth, "'If you can meet with Triumph and Disaster': Charles Krauthammer 1950–2018," at https://richardlangworth.com/charles-krauthammer-1950-2015, accessed June 20, 2020.

## Chapter 11 – The Exchange

1   Frank Sinatra, Sammy Cahn, and James Van Heusen, "Love and Marriage," Barton Music Corporation (ASCAP), 1955.

2   Alfred, Lord Tennyson, accessed June 20, 2020, https://knowledgenuts.com/2014/02/05/tennyson-wrote-tis-better-to-have-loved-and-lost-about-a-man.

3   Cory Ashbury, *Reckless Love* (Lake Mary, Florida: Charisma House, 2020), 7.

4   Mr. Rogers, accessed June 25, 2020, https://www.inc.com/geoffrey-james/45-quotes-from-mr-rogers-that-we-all-need-today.html.

5   Rob Holt, *What the Cross Means to Me* (Eugene, Oregon: Harvest House Publishers, 2002).

6   Calvin Miller, *Into the Depths of God* (Minneapolis, Minnesota: Bethany House Publishers, 2000), 215–216.

7   Ann Voskamp, *The Way of Abundance* (Grand Rapids, Michigan: Zondervan, 2018), 59.

## Chapter 12 – The Legacy

1   Billy Graham, accessed June 20, 2020, quoted from https://www.goodreads.com/quotes/846323-the-legacy-we-leave-is-not-just-in-our-possessions.
2   Calvin Miller, *Into the Depths of God* (Minneapolis, Minnesota, Bethany House Publishers, 2000), 140.
3   John Piper, *Desiring God,* accessed June 20, 2020, quoted from https://twitter.com/desiringGod/status/328924141560418305, April 29, 2013.
4   Anita Corrine Donihue, quoted by Ashleigh Bryce Clayton, *A Gentle Spirit* (Uhrichsville, Ohio: Barbour Publishing, Inc. 1999), from the April 22 reading.

## Chapter 13 – The End

1   Yogi Berra, *BBC Magazine*, accessed June 20, 2020 https://www.bbc.com/news/magazine-34324865#.
2   Robert "Tot" Calvert, *Atoka County Times,* Atoka, Oklahoma, January 9, 2014.
3   John Newton, "Amazing Grace," 1779, public domain.
4   Marilyn Hickey, *It's Not Over until You Win* (Englewood, CO: Marilyn Hickey Ministries, 2019).

## Chapter 14 – The Conclusion

1   Gloria Gaither, "It's Not about Now," Gaither Music Co., 2001.
2   Rick Warren, *The Purpose Driven Life* (Grand Rapids, Michigan: Zondervan, 2002), 38.

## Appendix A: The History

1   Beatrice Bayley, "History of Ethnic Origins," *Family Heritage Book* (Beatrice Bayley, Inc. Publisher). Additional reference: accessed on June 25, 2020, https://en.wikipedia.org/wiki/German _Americans #Texas.
2   Sadie Olene (Barrett) Walker and Karen Eileen (Barrett) Craig Lerma, *The Bode and Radetzky Families History*, unpublished manuscripts. Used by permission.
3   Ibid.
4   Ibid.
5   Ibid.
6   Accessed June 24, 2020: https://en.wikipedia.org/wiki/Joseph_Radetzky_von_Radetz.
7   Accessed June 24, 2020: https://en.wikipedia.org/wiki/Radetzky_March.

8   Accessed June 24, 2020: https://www.nm.cz/en/visit-us/buildings/lapidarium-of-the-national-museum.

9   Sadie Olene (Barrett) Walker and Karen Eileen (Barrett) Craig Lerma, *The Bode and Radetzky Families History*, unpublished manuscripts. Used by permission.

10  Ibid.

11  Ibid.

12  Ibid.

13  Centennial Committee, *Here's Harper* (Fredericksburg, Texas: The Radio Post, Inc. 1963), 3–5, 15, 47, 63.

14  Hubert Wesley and Howard Elton Lacey, *The William Lacy and Elliott Lacy Families of New Kent and Chesterfield Counties, Virginia* (Chelsea, Michigan: BookCrafters, 1996), vol. 1, no. 5.

15  Ibid.

16  Steve Green and Jon Mohr, "Find Us Faithful," published by Birdwing Music (ASCAP) and Jonathan Mark Music (ASCAP), 1987.

CPSIA information can be obtained
at www.ICGtesting.com
Printed in the USA
LVHW101107300922
729546LV00003B/5